THE NIGHTMARE BEGINS . . .

The library door opened and I heard footsteps approaching. The area in which I was standing was suddenly icy cold.

"Who's there?" I called out.

Silence. After a few tense seconds I heard footsteps pass right by me and start to mount the stairs.

"Who are you?" I tried to yell but my voice came out in a sort of croak. My challenge went unanswered as the footsteps continued their steady climb up the stairs to the third floor. I heard a door softly close. Then all was silent. . . .

**NIGHT
STALKS
THE
MANSION**

NIGHT STALKS THE MANSION

A True Story of One Family's Ghostly Adventure

BY CONSTANCE WESTBIE
AND HAROLD CAMERON

BANTAM BOOKS
TORONTO · NEW YORK · LONDON · SYDNEY

Certain place names relating to the events set forth in this book have been changed in order to protect the privacy of the present-day residents.

This low-priced Bantam Book has been completely reset in a type face designed for easy reading, and was printed from new plates. It contains the complete text of the original hard-cover edition.
NOT ONE WORD HAS BEEN OMITTED

NIGHT STALKS THE MANSION
A Bantam Book / published by arrangement with Stackpole Books

PRINTING HISTORY
Stackpole edition published March 1978
2nd printing . . . May 1978

Bantam edition / December 1978

2nd printing .. December 1978	7th printing . September 1979
3rd printing .. December 1978	8th printing . September 1979
4th printing ... January 1979	9th printing .... April 1980
5th printing ... January 1979	10th printing . December 1980
6th printing ... January 1979	11th printing ... January 1981
	12th printing ... March 1984

ISBN 0-553-14960-1

Published simultaneously in the United States and Canada

Bantam Books are published by Bantam Books, Inc. Its trademark, consisting of the words "Bantam Books" and the portrayal of a rooster, is Registered in U.S. Patent and Trademark Office and in other countries. Marca Registrada. Bantam Books, Inc., 666 Fifth Avenue, New York, New York 10103.

PRINTED IN THE UNITED STATES OF AMERICA

H   21 20 19 18 17 16 15 14 13 12

To Dorothy, beloved wife and mother, who shared our experiences in the house on Plum Tree Lane and who, even after passing into a higher realm of consciousness, has found ways to assure me of her continuing love and interest in my affairs, this book is affectionately dedicated.

—HAROLD W. CAMERON

Contents

Preface

This book results from a collaboration between two people: Harold Cameron and Constance Westbie. Harold and the rest of the Cameron family lived the story; Constance Westbie pieced it together from interviews and notes kept by Harold and from affidavits given by the children, relatives, and visitors to the Mansion.

Because of Harold Cameron's insistence that the story be presented truthfully, as fact and not fiction, and because the bizarre events and ghostly manifestations in the old house on Plum Tree Lane could well prove incredible to a sober-minded reader, the publisher offers the following testimony of Harold Cameron, verbatim:

It is significant, I think, that we never gave her a name. There was no inclination to bestow upon her a derisive or derogatory label. . . . Perhaps we were secretly a little afraid to do so because we speedily learned that she had a temper. Then, too, we came to hold her in esteem and respect. Judging from our impressions, she must have been a great lady in her day.

As for the other one—I admit we confused the two for a time. Yet his heavy footsteps on the graveled drive and the front porch of the old mansion were distinctive and not like hers at all. We soon realized, to our consternation, that we had not one, but two disembodied visitors who shared our residence and grounds on Plum Tree Lane for nearly two years.

As far as we know, they may still be there.

—THE PUBLISHER

1

The Gift Horse

> **For Lease:** Country Manor estate. House dating back to Revolutionary Days. Seventeen rooms. Completely furnished. Antiques. Grounds beautifully landscaped. Convenient location. Rich in historical background and atmosphere. A home for gracious entertaining. Reasonable terms for right tenant.

I put down the newspaper and looked around the crowded motel room: two double beds, three cots, open suitcases, packing boxes. This had been home for the Cameron clan—five children, myself, and my wife —for weeks since we left the West Coast. I had been transferred by my company at the end of World War II and had been sent to Philadelphia to start up an office and warehouse for our post-war operations.

1

We clearly had to move—and very soon! Dorothy, my wife, usually a model of competency and efficiency, was fed up with togetherness! Hal and Bob, our two college-age sons; Carrol, our ten-year-old; Janet, four years old and our only daughter; and Michael, our six-month-old infant, all desperately needed more living room.

Growing more and more excited, I read the ad to Dorothy.

"Seventeen rooms?" Dorothy echoed. "But we don't need seventeen rooms."

"Neither does anyone else. That's why we'll probably get it," I grinned. "Seventeen is better than none at all. You know how we've combed the country around Philadelphia. Housing is at a premium and there hasn't been anything to rent or lease. I've got to get located or get fired. We can't go on like this!" I indicated the disorder with a wave of my hand. "I'll check with the realtor on my way to the office. Better phone them that I'll be a few minutes late."

I tore the page out of the paper and stuffed it into my coat pocket, kissed Dorothy hastily on the cheek, and drove quickly to the real estate agency.

The broker was an immaculate, tidy-looking individual behind an untidy desk. He had gray hair, gray eyes, and a gray toothbrush moustache. I was enough of a salesman, myself, to recognize his swift appraisal of me. He was wondering whether or not I was a "live" prospect. I didn't keep him long in doubt.

"I'm Harold Cameron," I announced. "I'm with Aluminum Corporation of America with headquarters in Philadelphia and I need a house for a family of seven."

He was noncommittal until I showed him the ad that had brought me to his office. Then he brightened up considerably.

"Is this place still for lease?" I demanded.

"Yes, Mr. Cameron. Not everyone can appreciate a splendid old mansion or would be comfortable in a country estate." I recognized the sales pitch but it was what I'd expected.

"Tell me about it," I urged.

He went into an elaborate description of the old family dwelling which was appropriately called the mansion. He spoke in a clipped British accent and at times I was more interested in his voice than his words. I did learn, however, that the property was located seventeen miles out of Philadelphia in the suburb of Wynne, and was available for only $3600 per year on a two-year lease.

"This is less than half of its real leasing value," he informed me. "It's almost impossible to find anything for lease or rent around here since the war. This is a great bargain."

I saw no reason to tell him that I was so desperate that any house big enough to stretch in would be a great bargain. I was also intrigued by his mention of seven big fireplaces in the house and that it was completely furnished.

"About all that furniture," I began. "I could use some, of course, but I have a lot of my own in storage. I ordered it shipped out here when I was transferred from Portland. Then, too, I don't want to be responsible for the safety of valuable antiques in a household of kids."

"Anything you don't want can be stored with no problem," he promised.

The deal was sounding better all the time. "What about the plumbing?" I asked.

"It's in fine shape. No one has lived there for any length of time for years, but things like that have been kept up." Then he added as an afterthought, "The owners aren't exactly impoverished, you understand. They spend most of their time in Europe. Of course the place will need some renovating but if you are willing to sign a lease, that will be taken care of before you move in."

"When can I see the house?" I wanted to know.

He glanced at his watch. "Today? I have several appointments but maybe . . ."

"Later this afternoon. I'll take the family out to look it over. Do you have a key for me? Then we won't have to bother you if I'm delayed and can't keep a definite appointment."

He selected a big key from a pile in a desk drawer and held it out. "This unlocks the front door. I'll trust you with the key, Mr. Cameron. You don't look like a vandal. Just take your time looking the place over."

"What are the neighbors like?" I questioned as I got up to leave.

He gave me a curious look. "You won't be bothered with neighbors," he promised with a faint smile, "and they won't be bothered with you—not unless your ancestors beat the Mayflower over. Some relatives run the adjoining farm but they aren't too sociable as far as newcomers are concerned. None of these oldtimers are," he added reflectively.

"How long does one stay a newcomer?" I asked with interest.

"Oh, I venture to say about twenty or thirty years." He spoke quietly, but with a flash of humor.

"I'll contact you tomorrow," I promised.

Somehow I felt we were going to get that house. I was able to concentrate on a multitude of duties at the office that day without the subconscious worry that had nagged me about housing.

Dorothy and I thought alike. The very things I had

mentioned as possible obstacles to our leasing were the ones she brought up as we were on our way to inspect the premises later that afternoon. Hal and Bob were with us. I had given five dollars to the daughter of the motel manager to keep an eye on the younger children for an hour or so until our return.

"Harold—" Dorothy began hesitantly. "—about those antiques . . ."

"We're not baby-sitting with a bunch of antiques," I reassured her. "They will store them for the time of our lease, along with the furniture we don't want."

She laughed. "Well, that's a relief! I have enough baby-sitting to do in other areas."

"If only half of what he says is true, the place is a gift at that price," I observed. "I'm not looking a gift horse in the mouth."

It was an old saying that I came to disagree with a little too late. One should not only look a gift horse in the mouth but scrupulously examine every molar. There is always the danger that it could turn into a different breed of animal—the proverbial white elephant.

Dorothy had one more question. "What about plumbing in an old place like that?"

"Good shape. I asked about that."

Dorothy wasn't the type to raise too many objections before she inspected things for herself. Now she sighed a little and settled back to enjoy the drive.

Leaving industrial Philadelphia, we entered a different world—one of beauty and serenity, green rolling hills, clusters of trees, tidy farms and spacious dwellings. We had driven for twenty minutes and had just crossed a small stream when the mansion suddenly loomed before our eyes. It was a great house situated on a hill about a quarter of a mile away. I

was immediately impressed by its grandeur. Four jut-
ting chimneys thrust themselves above the third
floor level into the lowering clouds that darkened the
sky on that wintry Pennsylvania afternoon. A few
minutes later we approached the front drive which
swung into the property from Plum Tree Lane. A
stone fence had separated the extensive grounds from
the road for about three hundred yards. I stopped the
car on the circular drive at the front door.

"Will you look at that!"

"I am looking," Dorothy replied in a small voice. A
sharp whistle sounded from the back seat where
the boys were riding.

Constructed of gray Philadelphia granite, the mansion could have been used as an illustration for *The
Fall of the House of Usher*. A concrete veranda took
up about a third of the entire circumference of the
house, running from the front door around to the
kitchen entrance.

Awed at the sight, we climbed silently from the car
and walked up to the massive, carved walnut door
which opened readily with a turn of the key. We
found ourselves in a large entrance hall. Directly before us a wide stairway curved up to the second
floor. At our left a door opened into the living room
which held furniture draped with heavy cloth dusters.
I felt I had stepped backward in time.

Dorothy ran an investigating finger over a shrouded
chair and promptly sneezed. Dust settled in a gray
film over everything in the room.

"Gosh!" Bob exclaimed. "It's like being in King Tut's
tomb!"

"That would be nice clean dirt compared to this,"
Dorothy replied a little grimly.

"Why, Mom!" Hal observed with a grin. "That's the

first time I ever heard you admit there was such a thing as clean dirt!"

Dorothy wasn't in the mood for levity. She sneezed again and reached for a tissue.

Against the back wall and facing the entrance was a large walk-in fireplace that could easily accommodate a six-foot log. We went through wide French doors into a dining room as impressive in size as the living room and found another fireplace of identical dimensions.

"At least we'd have heat," I laughed. Privately, I loved the old fireplaces even though I knew we might use them very little.

"Provided there's enough timber left in this neck of the woods to keep them burning," Bob replied. "I'd hate to have to cut wood for Dad's heat!"

From the rear of the dining room we walked into a big, old-fashioned kitchen where we started opening doors. One disclosed stairs to the servants' quarters above; another opened on a stairway to the basement which, in itself, contained seven rooms (these were in addition to the seventeen mentioned in the real estate ad). A third door led to a stairwell in the back yard and it was securely locked. Still another one opened into the butler's pantry and that, in turn, was provided with its own exit under the broad stairway that faced the front door. We found ourselves back in the entrance hall where we had started.

Dorothy had stopped sneezing and was very quiet. "Which way now?" she asked simply.

I led the way through a short hallway to the right with a great sliding door of heavy oak at its end. Pushing it open, we discovered a library at least twenty-five feet wide that extended to the back of the house and had its own exit into the back yard. Filled bookshelves, at least five feet tall, extended around three sides of the room except where deep windows with built-in seats were set into the walls.

"They built houses to last in those days, Dad." Hal was measuring the depth of the stone walls with his arm.

I welcomed his comment as it distracted Dorothy from her silent contemplation of those bookshelves. I knew she was thinking that just keeping the books dusted would be a job in itself. There was another immense fireplace in the library. Two old long barreled hunting rifles, like the ones used by pioneers, were crossed above the mantel like medieval swords. A long antique davenport was placed in front of the fireplace. Behind it was an old-fashioned library table with a lamp for reading before the fire. Two crystal chandeliers gave an ornate touch to what once must have been an elegant and charming room.

Dorothy's mood had changed almost imperceptibly. "You know," she said softly, "the Prince might have felt this way when he entered the palace to awaken Sleeping Beauty. Life seems to have just been suspended for some reason or other."

"I feel it, too," I agreed.

We trooped upstairs. Here were bedrooms and several baths, all in remarkably good condition. Most impressive of all was the master bedroom which was located directly above the library and had the same measurements. Through an alcove we looked into a smaller adjoining room that might have served as an upstairs sitting or sewing room but which would serve very well as a nursery for Janet and Michael. There were additional rooms on the third floor, but we didn't go up there. Darkness was gathering swiftly and there was no electricity in the house. We still wanted to see the grounds in what was left of the daylight.

Outside, at the right rear of the mansion, was the old summerhouse, overgrown with climbing roses and honeysuckle. I'm not usually a romantic, but I did wonder fleetingly how many "sweet nothings" had been whispered here in moonlit moments of the past.

"Oh, Harold! Just look at that maple!" Dorothy cried out.

Some thirty feet away grew the largest and most beautiful red maple I had ever seen. Its lower branches nearly touched the ground and when leafed out, it would make a bower larger than the summerhouse itself. I couldn't even venture a guess at its age but it looked ancient.

We walked, single file, down the drive and past the kitchen, to an old coach house. No coaches remained, but it wouldn't have surprised any of us to hear a ghostly whinny. There were ancient pieces of tattered harness on the walls, a bridle with rusted bits and shrunken leather, and two horse collars covered with cobwebs, the leather stiffened and hard as stone.

The shadowy coach house was an eerie place at best, but Bob was irrepressible. He caroled softly, "Old Faithful, we roamed the range together . . ."

"You're not back in New Mexico, kid," Hal laughed. We had lived in that state when the boys were younger and they had learned to ride horses and rope cattle. "No cowpoke's pony ever munched oats in these stalls."

"He's right," I put in. "Hunters and gaited carriage stock were cared for here."

It was so dark that we were forced to end our inspection tour. This I did reluctantly because the house and grounds were exerting a terrific emotional pull and I was falling under a spell from the past that I had never felt before. It was as if I was *supposed* to be in that house; I *must* walk over the grounds; listen to a message from the past. I didn't understand my reaction and couldn't explain it. It was so foreign to my usual manner of thinking that I couldn't even speak. I relocked the front door and we climbed back into the car. Then I turned to Dorothy who took a deep breath like a swimmer coming up for air.

"I could never keep that house up properly," she finally said.

"You'll have help," I pointed out. "We'll also close off the top floor entirely. We don't need it."

"The kitchen is impossible!"

I knew my wife very well. She was clean and meticulous and very particular about her kitchen. When she said this one was impossible, I knew she was really telling me that it was going to be impossible to get her into it.

"We'll have a new modern kitchen," I promised. "You'll be surprised what a good cleaning and a new paint job will do for the whole place."

She must have been remembering the historical account of Washington's winter at Valley Forge which wasn't too far away from Wynne. "What about the furnace?" she demanded. "It might have been suitable when the house was filled with servants, but who will stoke it this winter?"

I had already made a mental note about the furnace. "Not you, honey, and not me. I'll insist on a new oil burner grate being installed in the basement."

After a moment of silence she turned to me with real puzzlement in her voice. "You really *like* this house, don't you, Harold?"

"Yes, I do," I said flatly.

"But do you think they'll go to all of that work for us? We won't be paying much rent for a place like this if they do."

"They'll do it," I replied confidently. Again there was that feeling of inevitability. I was going to live in that house, come what may. "Houses have to be lived in and this one has been empty a long time."

"I wonder why?" she questioned, half to herself.

"It's rather obvious, isn't it? Just too much house for the average family. We don't want to buy it—we only want to lease for a couple of years. It would be an interesting experience—just living here for a while." My words were more prophetic than I realized at the time.

As she still didn't reply, I went on persuasively, "The owners want to lease this now. They want to improve the place and have it looked after by good tenants. They'll do what I ask."

The boys had been quiet in the back seat. They realized as well as I that the final decision must rest with their mother.

"Well," she admitted at last, "I'm tired of living out of a suitcase. I'm tired of no room at all. We have to settle down somewhere near Philadelphia and we certainly haven't found anything else. The country is pretty enough."

I held my breath as she went on musingly. "I hadn't expected anything quite so . . . so. . . ." Words failed her for a moment and then she went on resolutely. "I wasn't looking for anything so grand and overwhelming, but if the owners will meet your terms and you really want it as much as you seem to, I'll go along."

There were whoops of joy from both boys. They, too, had been impressed with the mansion and it would lend itself readily to entertaining their college friends during vacation periods and over special weekends.

Hal chuckled. "We could always turn it into a hotel if we got hard up."

"I'll feel like the King of England," Bob put in.

"Which one?" his mother wanted to know. "Edward VI?"

"Oh, come now," I laughed, relieved that we had finally reached a decision. "The place isn't that old!"

"Wanta bet?" Bob chuckled.

I looked up at the dark shape looming above our heads in the moonlight.

"Not really," I admitted as I turned the car toward town.

I was excited that night and didn't sleep well. However, I was calm enough when I presented myself at the real estate office the next morning. I expected a little argument over my demands and was braced for it. But surprisingly enough, the realtor, Mr. Reginald Petre-Wymer Brooks, promptly agreed that a new paint job was needed, a thorough cleaning from top to bottom, plus kitchen renovation and an up-to-date heating system. He assured me that these things would be specified in the lease that would be ready for my signature the following day. He also stated that the work would start immediately and that the place would be ready for occupancy in thirty days.

The next afternoon Dorothy and I were in the office for the signing of the lease. I had heard about Philadelphia lawyers and the lease was drawn up by one. I'm a pretty good businessman and I read the fine print. It was what was written in big print that I didn't pay enough attention to. I remember thinking that the lease was unusually binding, but that was what I wanted at the moment. I didn't intend to go through another house hunting session for at least two years and I seemed to have ample protection against a rise in rent after the renovations were completed and we were comfortably settled.

Feeling that I had struck a good bargain and could now turn my attention exclusively to earning my salary, I signed the lease with a happy flourish of the pen.

"I can forget this mess now," I told Dorothy back at the motel where she was preparing the evening meal for Michael. "I'll be too busy from now on to let it bother me—but I know the waiting will be hard on you."

"I'll manage," she assured me. "You can stand anything when you know it isn't permanent."

I was to remember that remark.

During the ensuing month we occasionally drove by the mansion where trucks and carpenters' supplies in the driveway indicated that work was going according to plan. Once or twice I stuck my head in and satisfied myself that there was no stalling on the job and that we'd be able to move in as promised. In the meantime we were free to use the basement for storage of things we had no pressing need for and that was a help.

"I'd rather do the final cleaning up, myself," Dorothy announced one day. "The boys can help me."

Her words didn't surprise me. Very few cleaning women had ever completely satisfied her.

When I could spare the time, which wasn't often, we drove around and tried to familiarize ourselves with the neighborhood. About the only information we succeeded in obtaining was geographical. I

learned what roads to avoid and which offered a
short cut to the highway. Regarding the occupants of
the other impressive homes in the area, we picked up
odds and ends of information from tradesmen, but I
gained the most knowledge from inquiries that I
made in Philadelphia. I did learn that the house was
something of a landmark. The local drugstore sold
post cards of it!

Bob hadn't been too far off base when he had mentioned royalty—and neither had the broker when he
assured me that no one would bother with us. I discovered that we were in the midst of a section even
more exclusive than Philadelphia's famous Main
Line. Our neighbors were referred to as "The Horsy
Crowd." They still followed tradition; they still had
fox hunts. Here dwelt the real elite—more than a step
above the nouveau riche that made up part of the
Main Line social register. For this reason there was no
near neighbor I could comfortably call upon to pass
the time of day and learn something about the history
of our old mansion. It would have required an en-
graved invitation to get me past the butler.

"You are a lucky man," Dorothy observed one afternoon when we had watched a front door being
opened by a black man in livery while a chauffeur
drove a black Rolls-Royce around to the rear of the
house. "I could be eating my poor heart out with a
yearning to be noticed. How nice that five children
keep me from having social ambitions!"

"I planned it that way," I told her with mock
solemnity.

The day finally arrived when everything was ready
for my final inspection. We were to move in the following morning when the electricity would be turned
on. I was again delayed at the office and it was early
evening when we drove up to see the final results of

the renovating job. All physical evidence of the carpenters and other workmen had been removed and the yard was orderly. I parked the car in the driveway and left the headlights on so that they focused on the front porch. It was dusk. I would have preferred more daylight in which to examine the work, but I had noted the progress to date was satisfactory and thought I could still give the kitchen and furnace room a quick look.

"Wait in the car," I told Dorothy. "I'll only be a minute."

Hal and Bob had accompanied us but they wanted to explore the grounds again so I was alone when I unlocked the front door and stepped inside. I could dimly see the hall extending back by the stairway with the butler's pantry door at its end. A quick glance showed the library door to be closed. I struck a few matches and inspected the paint job. All was in order. In the dining room, I scratched matches in succession at the fireplace and on a window ledge as the fast-receding daylight didn't permit too close a look. I wasn't too worried. I was already convinced that the workmen were careful and skilled.

The kitchen was a joy to behold. It was all new. The built-in ovens, freshly painted walls and stainless steel equipment glowed in the matchlight as though welcoming me into a modern miracle. This was the room that Dorothy had worried about and I was tempted to bring her in to see it but it was too dark for her to risk stumbling with Michael in her arms. Besides, I wanted to be sure that the furnace had been properly changed as agreed.

In the basement I proceeded cautiously. The furnace was in the third room back and there was no light to guide me. When I opened the furnace door, the air rushing out extinguished the match I was

holding. For a moment I panicked as I realized it was
the last match in the book. I stood there in the darkness frantically feeling in my pockets for another book
of matches and, to my immense relief, found one.
With the first flare of the new match I saw that everything was in order. Then I made my way back up
the stairs to the kitchen as fast as I safely could. I
started for the front door. It was then that I heard
the library door open and heard the approaching
footsteps.

"Who's there?" I called out.

There was no answer and I was annoyed. Although
my two sons had gone in different directions after
they scrambled from the car—one racing to the summerhouse and the other to the old coach house—I
was sure that one of them had come in while I was
checking on the new furnace installation in the basement, and was playing a trick on me.

I struck a match. I could see no one. Yet the library
door that I was so sure had been closed when I entered the premises was now open—and beyond it only
darkness.

The match flickered and died. Then I heard the
footsteps coming from the library toward the bottom
of the stairs that wound above me into the upper hall.
Again I struck a match and, again, there was no one
there.

"Hal?" I questioned tentatively. "Bob?"

Silence. After a few tense seconds, I heard the footsteps start to mount the stairs and I knew then that
they were not the footsteps of either boy. They were,
unmistakably, the footsteps of a woman with slippers
on her feet—the kind that Dorothy would have referred to as "mules." The soft flapping of the heels
could be heard distinctly as she went on up the stairs.

I had stepped forward and could have reached

through the railings and grasped her ankle as she passed, but I couldn't have moved my hand to do so if my life depended on it. The area in which I was standing was suddenly icy cold.

"Who are you?" I yelled. At least I thought I was yelling, but my voice came out in a sort of croak as it does in a nightmare. I wasn't too sure that I wasn't having one, either—and would soon be feeling a sharp jab from my wife's elbow in my ribs. I reached for the newel post and felt the wood—cold and solid —beneath my hand. I had to be awake!

I yelled again.

My challenges went unanswered. There wasn't the slightest change in the rhythm of the footsteps as they continued their steady climb up the stairs. I stood, dumfounded, as I heard them in the upper hall. They went on up to the third floor. I heard a door softly close and all was silent.

I finally moved . . . fast. I stumbled out the front door where the porch was brightened by the head-lights of the car—a most welcome sight.

Dorothy, with Michael in her lap, was waiting for me where I had left her. The two older boys were rummaging in the yard. I could hear their voices. We had dropped Carrol and Janet off earlier to see a movie and were to pick them up on our way home. My family was accounted for. None of them had entered the house.

The boys had come running when I yelled. "Some-one is in the house!" I shouted now.

"Who?" Hal demanded in amazement.

"That's what we're going to find out," I promised grimly.

I took a flashlight from the glove compartment, regretting that I hadn't had it before. True, I had seen nothing by matchlight in the dark hall, but a heavy concentrated beam most certainly would have shown up the woman on the stairs. Who was she? What was she doing in our house? She was an intruder and had no business there. We were going to confront her and demand an explanation.

I didn't tell them that I thought it was a woman. This had only been my impression. It might have been a man wearing oversized slippers. Hal picked up a tire iron and Bob grabbed a bigger flashlight that we used on camping trips and kept in the trunk of the car with other tools. Then the three of us went back into the house. I glanced back and saw that Dorothy was locking the car from the inside.

"Dad, are you *sure?*" Bob hesitated at the foot of the stairs.

"Of course, I'm sure!" My voice was sharper than I intended because I was still uneasy. I led the way up to the third floor. We went through bedrooms and closets and checked adjoining baths. We found only one locked door leading into the hall.

"Open up!" I yelled, pounding on the closed door. "I know you're in there!"

There was no answer. The only sound was the echo of my voice in the empty hall. My elation that we had finally trapped the culprit was shortlived. We walked into the room through an adjoining one and found it empty. Then we inspected the rest of the house and tested all doors leading to the outside. They were securely locked. Finally we went slowly back to the car.

"While you were waiting, did you notice anything unusual?" I asked Dorothy. "Did you see anyone go into the house—or run out?"

"Of course not," she replied a little impatiently. "The headlights were on all the time, too. What *is* the matter with you, Harold?"

By that time I wasn't sure. Maybe I had been working too hard and needed a rest. Perhaps I had only imagined the footsteps. The whole atmosphere of the old mansion was eerie at night and would certainly encourage fearful impressions. But I had never been possessed of an overactive imagination. I was a practical person, used to dealing with facts and figures. Then I thought again of that library door. Could I have only thought that it was closed when I first entered the hall? Had I *really* heard it open? I was completely confused.

I didn't have much to say on our way back to town. I was too busy with my own chaotic thoughts. I certainly had been convinced that an intruder was in the house. But, if so, why the silence at my challenge? Where did she go? Why the mystery? I didn't want to discuss it further at the moment for it would only make Dorothy unduly nervous. And it didn't help my frame of mind to hear occasional chuckles from the back seat. I realized, then, that the boys had never felt that there was really anyone in the house at all.

The next morning I phoned Mr. Brooks and asked if there was an extra set of keys to the place. I told him I was sure someone had been in the house the previous night.

He seemed puzzled. "The foreman turned in all the keys," he informed me. "You have them. I don't even have a set, myself. Was there any sign of a forced entry?"

"None."

"Well, if there was someone," and his voice indicated that he doubted it, "they have gone by now. No one will camp out there when a big family is moving in."

I hung up, impressed by his logic. It would take a

foolhardy intruder to remain in hiding when the Camerons took up residence.

The general manager of our firm was in Philadelphia that week for a visit. I told him, jokingly, of my experience and waited for him to share the laugh. Instead, he just gave me a strange look.

"I'd get out of that lease if I were you," he said with a seriousness that astounded me. "When we drove past the house the other day, it gave me the creeps. Sure you want a place that big?"

For a moment I felt a twinge of apprehension, but it soon passed. In the bright light of day I had begun to doubt the reality of my impressions. Everything had to have a logical explanation and I felt I'd find one in this instance. Besides, I was still captivated by the aura that surrounded the imposing ancestral mansion. While growing up, historical novels had been my preference and the place looked like it had been the setting for one. Also, not to be overlooked, there was the new kitchen, new paint job and the new furnace—all renovated according to my specifications. There was also the signed lease. I told myself that the Camerons were a normal, noisy bunch and that all would be well. Dorothy was already packed and so were the boys. I decided to be my usual sensible self.

"Sure, I'm sure," I laughed.

And so we moved into the house on Plum Tree Lane.

2
Initiation

There followed the usual flurry of activity that accompanies moving and getting settled. Surplus furniture was stored in a big barn located on adjacent holdings known as "The Farm." Here lived some of those "poor" relatives that Brooks had spoken of. The Farm consisted of two or three sections of land on which was a large farmhouse, several out-buildings and the barn which was only about a quarter of a mile away from the mansion. The relatives didn't encourage intimacy and we, in turn, didn't desire it, so we got along without trouble.

I had registered with an employment agency in town, asking for a couple who would live in. The woman was to help with the housework and the man would take care of the yard and do odd jobs. I wanted references, of course. Perhaps that's why it took so long to hear from interested applicants. In the meantime Dorothy swept, scrubbed, vacuumed, dusted and polished. The boys good-naturedly lent a hand with the heavy work although their patience wore a bit thin before their mother had finally moved and arranged furniture to her satisfaction. Then we all had to agree that the old mansion looked equally impressive, inside and out.

"There's one good thing about this house," Dorothy announced triumphantly. "Responsibility for a messy bathroom can no longer be shifted to the shoulders of the innocent!"

There were several bedrooms and baths on the upper floors. I had always done my share of business entertaining and we had numerous relatives who visited periodically. It was going to be a relief to put up groups without having anyone feel the visit was an imposition or having family members stay at the closest motel. We were congratulating ourselves on the fact that we had made a good choice of a home when an unexpected problem developed. *Someone else heard footsteps in the night!*

We'd been there about two weeks when Hal woke from a sound sleep and heard someone walking down the hall shortly after midnight. He grinned to himself, remembering some leftover chicken and half a lemon pie in the refrigerator and decided that Bob wasn't going to enjoy a private raid by himself. He swung out of bed and followed to the head of the stairs and then stopped, puzzled. There was no light on downstairs. He went back to Bob's room, opened the door and looked in. Bob was sitting up in bed, his dark hair disheveled. When he saw Hal, he gave a sigh of relief.

"Oh, it's only you," he said. "I thought . . . well, I thought it was something else."

"Didn't you just get out of bed and go down the hall?" Hal demanded.

"Who, me? Not on your life!"

"That's funny. I heard somebody but there are no lights on downstairs. Let's see where Dad is."

Together they came into our bedroom where Dad was asleep, but not for long. Dorothy, like all mothers, slept in that no man's land between physical rest and subconscious awareness that woke her immediately at the slightest whimper from a child. She sat up in bed and turned on the light while I blinked sleepily.

I listened to their story and could only shake my head. "You kids will be okay," I said, reassuringly. "No one can be in the house. We'll check on Carrol."

The younger boy was fast asleep, the covers over his head. I accompanied his brothers back to their respective rooms. Then I went back to Dorothy who was waiting for me, perturbed.

"Did you find anything?" she questioned.

"Not a thing."

"Hum!" Then she faced me suddenly. "Harold, did you really hear footsteps in the house that night before we moved in?"

I was uncomfortable. "I thought I did at the time," I admitted reluctantly.

"And now?"

"Well, I've just put it all out of my mind," I assured her.

"Maybe you'd better just put it back in," she said thoughtfully. "Hal isn't the nervous type and he isn't afraid of anything. If it had been only Bob now, I wouldn't think so much about it. But both of them . . ."

"I know," I agreed. "I'm as puzzled as you are. We'll just have to wait and see what else happens—if anything does."

She slid out of bed and went into the nursery to look in on Michael and Janet. Everything was okay there, so she climbed back into bed. "Well, there's nothing we can do about it tonight. Let's try and get some sleep."

I had never admired her more. Dorothy was a calm, unexcitable person who created scarcely a ripple on the smooth pond of family existence as she moved serenely through her busy days. She was the ideal wife for a tense, hard-driving business executive. Just to be near her would quiet me down after a hectic day at the Philadelphia office or a quick trip to my other headquarters in Washington or New York. Tonight, however, I could have understood an emotional outburst but she had surprised even me. I leaned over and kissed her.

"I love you, Dorothy."

We had agreed to wait and see what happened. We didn't have to wait long. A new element was added. It wasn't a new composition exactly—merely a variation on the original theme. Footsteps, measured and dignified, no longer confined themselves to the upper halls, stairway and library. They entered each bedroom in turn and the occupants seemed to be subjected to some sort of scrutiny.

The first time it happened, Dorothy and I both heard the footsteps approach our bed. Someone stood there, unseen in the darkness, but certainly felt. Then the steps receded into the hall although we were unaware of the door being opened.

"Harold," Dorothy whispered, nudging me a little.

I was shaken. "I know," I whispered back, turning on the light. "I heard it, too."

"What does it mean?"

"I don't pretend to know." The room was empty and completely normal.

"What can we do?"

"Nothing at the moment. Let's not alarm the kids."

But it wasn't long before we were forced to compare notes as the three boys, in turn, spoke of the phenomenon.

"Gosh, Mom!" Carrol cried, his eyes big in his sensitive little face. "Wasn't that you, last night? I sure thought it was. I even asked what you wanted but when you didn't answer, I thought you'd gone out. So I just went back to sleep."

When the boys discovered that they had all experienced the same sort of visitation, they held a hurried conference and decided to sleep together in one room. It was a large enough room for the three beds as Carrol's was little more than a cot. There was still room for a chair or two and a study desk as well as a small bookcase.

Bob announced their plans later in the day. "We're worried about Carrol sleeping in a room all by himself," he confided.

I suppressed a smile. "So it will take both of you to keep him company?"

He nodded, a little sheepishly. "We guess so."

Even this arrangement was changed. The ghostly inspections continued and a few days later, without further explanation, or even asking our permission, the boys dragged their mattresses into our master bedroom and slept on the floor for several nights. Later on they returned to their original rooms for dressing and studying, but when night came, the three of them slept together in Carrol's room for the balance of our stay on Plum Tree Lane.

I had never been a man who took family problems to his office. I was in a competitive business and couldn't afford to be contemplating mysterious footsteps and unseen visitors at work. When I turned the car out of our driveway in the morning, I was already thinking of my first appointment of the day; of the list of "things to do" scribbled on my desk calendar. But I had never before been faced with a situation like this. I got in the habit of driving slowly and looking back at the house while I breathed a prayer.

"Keep them safe, God, until I get home."

It didn't occur to me for quite a while that my prayer was a little vainglorious. I was actually telling the Almighty to keep them safe and when I got home I, Harold Cameron, would handle things! As a matter of fact, I handled nothing.

That next week we became aware of another manifestation. Again it was a variation on the basic theme, this time in bass notes. Another set of footsteps was heard on the gravel drive outside the house. They came from the area around the old coach house and were clearly discernible as they approached the house and went up the steps to the front door. Then the sound would abruptly cease. We were to remember later on that they would be particularly noticeable when the moon was bright and the air clear.

Again we convened a family meeting.

"They aren't the same ones, Dad," Hal said positively. "These are heavy—like a big man sort of pounding along on the gravel—I can hear it crunch under his feet."

"But no feet," Bob added wryly.

Again we talked and speculated. Again we could do nothing about the situation. The unseen lady who moved about the mansion gave the impression of dignity and seemed to mind her own business, whatever it was. Her footsteps, always identified by the steady rhythm and whispering scuff of slippers, never left the inside of the house. After she walked from the library at night, she climbed steadily to the third floor. On the other hand, there was something ominous about the man's footsteps as they crunched down upon the graveled drive and climbed the front steps. They made us uneasy. It didn't contribute to my peace of mind to read in occult literature that often an evil entity could be detected by an unpleasant odor, for this was the next stage of our developing drama.

I was awakened one night by a hard jab in the ribs from Dorothy. "Wake up, Harold! What is that awful smell?"

It had been a hard day. I had arrived by plane from Washington at the Philadelphia airport, grabbed a hurried meal because I was too late for dinner and had driven home completely bushed. I was still half-asleep.

"Maybe it's coming from the nursery," I muttered drowsily.

The words were unfortunate. "Nursery?" she echoed, aghast. "My babies never smelled like that in their whole lives!"

She jabbed me again and this time it really hurt. I came awake fast, took a good sniff, and nearly choked.

I have never been able to adequately describe that odor. It was pungent, acrid and strong. The nearest thing to it was creosote, but it was much more unpleasant. It seemed to be held like a foul blanket above our heads and then pressed down until we were nearly suffocated.

That first night we experienced it I jumped out of bed, switched on the light and ran to open a window. Then I stopped, utterly astonished, and beckoned for Dorothy to join me. She did so and we stared at each other.

"It's gone!" she cried.

I nodded. There wasn't the slightest trace of the odor where we stood. We approached the bed and were immediately engulfed by it. The only comparison I could make would be that of a powerful spotlight if it were shedding odor instead of light. It concentrated on a single area. We could move in or out of the condensed essence at will. Usually it was focused from above onto our bed. Sometimes, however, if one of us were reading in a chair, it would suddenly descend without warning. Once it was "set" it didn't shift around but remained in place until the essence or energy was spent. Later, I remembered comparing it to a lawn sprinkler placed in position and left to do its work while the gardener went about other chores, only to have its mechanism shut it off after sufficient time had elapsed. In our case the ensuing time was enough to worry us, make us physically uncomfortable, and do away with sleep.

I sat in a big armchair against the wall that first time for about forty-five minutes, holding Dorothy on my lap. She was tense and I was frustrated, for a sense of personal guilt was growing—I had been the one who insisted on bringing her into this house. Eventually the stench disappeared. When the room cleared we went back to bed but not to sleep.

I lay awake and thought of my youthful days when I'd been a student at a Baptist seminary in New Mexico. I had wanted to be a preacher like my dad and had finished the academic work and had preached a sermon for the faculty when my world caved in. Although I thought I'd done well, I was quickly challenged by the dean.

"You don't seem to believe in hell, Harold," he stated sternly. "Do you?"

Until that moment I hadn't realized how much I had mentally rejected certain rigid orthodox beliefs. I was faced with my moment of truth.

"Not in the kind you do, I guess," I admitted. Privately, I thought the reason many people liked to believe in hell was because they had acquaintances they'd like to see consigned there. The dean questioned me ruthlessly about other commonly accepted dogma and tried to "turn my wagon around" as he put it. The effort was not successful; I couldn't lie to please him and still retain my self-respect. After the interview, I was requested to withdraw from the seminary. After a few tears shed in private, I resigned formally and gave up all plans for the ministry. Turning my back on organized religion, I started looking for a job.

To my surprise I discovered that I really enjoyed the business world and my advancement was rapid. After I started with Montgomery Ward, it was only a matter of months until I was promoted from salesman to assistant sales manager with seventy employees under me. I then went to work for other concerns and ended up with Aluminum Corporation of America as sales manager with contacts on both sides of the Atlantic. Although I was considered successful and my work was demanding and interesting, sometimes the memory of that early rejection by the dean still rankled. Once I admitted as much to Dad.

"I really thought God had touched me on the shoulder," I told him.

Dad understood. "He touches a lot of people on the shoulder but it doesn't always mean that they are to preach the gospel. Living it is more important, to my way of thinking."

There had been nothing in my seminary training to prepare me to deal with ghosts. All psychic phenomena were lumped under "manifestations of the devil." But if this was true, why had the Camerons been singled out from all my other acquaintances for such visitations? Lying awake in that huge four-poster bed in the old mansion in Pennsylvania, I thought if those fumes had been sulfuric, I would have owed the old dean an apology.

Dorothy thumped her pillow and I realized that she hadn't been sleeping, either. "I don't know what that thing was," she finally commented. "But I'm going to spray this room tomorrow!"

"Do you think it will do any good?" I asked glumly.

"I don't know. But I have to do something!"

My reminiscences must have softened me somewhat. "Maybe we should start praying about what's going on around here."

She was silent for a moment. "I haven't heard you talk about prayer for quite a while," she observed. Then she gave a little chuckle. "Well, you pray and I'll spray!" She turned over to go to sleep.

Dorothy kept her word and thoroughly cleaned and fumigated the bedroom the next day, but that night there was the same jab in my ribs.

"Harold, it's back!"

It certainly was. We were again forced to the window and followed the same routine as the night before. This time we had to stay out of our bed for nearly two hours. I was tired and irritable the next morning due to interrupted sleep and plain confusion. I didn't understand what was happening. I couldn't cope. There was no one I could go to for advice without having them think I was crazy. But what was I to do?

We went on like this for several nights and my tension increased. My work at the office was showing the result of my abstraction. We couldn't continue like this indefinitely. Dorothy's face was showing strain and there were violet shadows under her eyes. One morning she sat down at the breakfast table and stared at me silently for a moment.

"I've had it, Harold!" she finally announced. "I know what we're up against in trying to find another place and I know how expensive the move will be—but at least I know what we're up against! That's more than I know here. I wonder if the place hadn't rented because tenants were scared away. I could never understand why you were so crazy about this house!"

It was the nearest to a "I told you so" that Dorothy ever permitted herself. When I didn't reply at once, she went on urgently. "You're going to see Mr. Brooks, aren't you? You've got to break our lease!"

I needed no further persuasion. "I intend to do just that," I answered grimly. After all, enough was enough!

I'd hate to have to write a do-it-yourself pamphlet on how to break a lease with the excuses I was forced to use that day. My arguments lost a little steam when I faced the meticulous Mr. Brooks once more across his littered desk and said what I had come to say. I had hoped my reputation as a level-headed businessman would help. It didn't seem to. He listened to my grievances in complete silence. The silence lasted so long that I felt my face getting hot.

"Well—it's the truth," I blurted out. "I have witnesses!"

"Perhaps it is, Mr. Cameron." Later I thought that he hadn't acted as amazed as I had expected. I wondered fleetingly if he had been expecting me.

"I'm getting out," I stated flatly.

"Certainly you may get out," he agreed smoothly. My relief at his words was short-lived as he went on emphatically. "Out of the house, that is, but not out of the lease. You had better make sure you understand your financial commitment."

He went over to his files and brought out a copy of the lease. I listened glumly as he read in his precise voice.

The terms of this lease are absolutely binding upon all parties. Under no circumstances shall said lease be terminated before the expiration date specified herein. The premises herein-described are not to be subleased. In the event that, for any reason whatever, the lessee shall vacate said premises, the rental payment of Three Hundred ($300.00) Dollars per month is still due and payable on the first day of each and every month until said expiration date. The lessee may, however, at his option, pay the entire balance due hereunder in one lump sun upon vacating said premises.

I was furious but part of my mind still functioned logically. I felt that a cold perusal of that lease might indicate that the lessor had actually anticipated an attempt to invalidate it.

"I'll get a lawyer," I threatened after a short silence.

"What do you suppose I got?" Brooks countered neatly. "You don't think I wrote the lease up by myself, do you?"

"You seem pretty adamant and unconcerned about all this! What personal ax are you grinding?" I sounded nasty and I intended to.

He only shrugged. "I represent the owners," he replied laconically. "When I'm given a job to do, I do it. You, of all people, should understand that, Mr. Cameron."

I wasn't quite through. "What about the fraudulent circumstances under which the lease was signed?" I demanded irately. "Nothing was said about having to share the premises with tenants already there."

He had the parting shot and it stopped me in my tracks. "Can you *prove* that there are other tenants in your house? Can you prove it in a court of law? That's what it would come to."

The horrifying vision of newspaper publicity and the ensuing reaction of my business associates if the matter came to court rendered me speechless—but I could still move. I slammed out the door.

I sat in the car until I had cooled down enough to think coherently. I had access to legal advice through my firm. However, I knew how fast rumors could fly through the office and I was reluctant to admit that I not only believed in ghosts but that I was being pestered by them. I'd put off that step as long as I could.

I went into a corner drugstore with a small breakfast bar and ordered a cup of coffee while I did some more thinking. I made no excuses for myself. I had jumped the gun. My own negligence now contributed to our present problems. I had always assured my salesmen that every problem carried within it the solution if you could figure it out. I did some figuring, myself, but I couldn't see any acceptable solution. Maybe I had overlooked some important factor. Maybe the answer was staring me in the face.

I looked up another attorney who had no connection with Brooks or his office. To my dismay, he gave me the same advice.

"No one can force you to stay, Mr. Cameron," he said, looking at me over the top of his bifocals after he had read the lease thoughtfully. "But you'll have to pay if you leave. Didn't you realize you'd be in a bind if your office transferred you to another city?"

"I didn't think about it," I admitted shortly. "My mind went on a vacation about that time." I hadn't gone into details as to my reasons for wanting to terminate the lease but had merely stated that private matters made it mandatory that I move.

"Sorry," he announced regretfully. "The lease is airtight and you signed it."

I left his office a defeated man.

That night I called yet another family conference. I included Carrol because, although barely ten, he knew what was going on and had already been in on certain ghostly visitations.

The entire family listened attentively as I told about the two unsuccessful visits of the morning—and what had motivated them.

"So there you have it," I announced wearily. "It isn't that we're scared—it's just that this is a darned nuisance and I don't have time to cope with it. We're in trouble and what are we going to do?"

Bob looked gloomy as his imagination took over. "We're all in a predicament," he said. "There goes Bob Cameron whose father is being chased by ghosts!"

"I seem to remember you boys running more than I did," I reminded him rather caustically.

"Sure," he agreed. "But that won't be in the papers."

"It will if this comes to court. You'll all be witnesses —even Carrol."

Hal was less voluble than Bob but what he said usually made sense. Now he spoke thoughtfully, his hazel eyes narrowed in concentration.

"Dad, none of us have been hurt—physically hurt —by these things. Maybe we can find out something about psychic phenomena and learn how to cope. I know there is such a thing even though none of us have been exposed to it before. Maybe we can learn about these things. Maybe we should learn about them. In the meantime, as I said, we haven't been hurt!"

"Only our feelings," Dorothy put in, sotto voce.

I agreed with her. Then I went on soberly. "Hal, you're right on both issues. To date these things have been—as I said before—only a nuisance. And we should learn more about this area."

"I don't think we're going to be hurt in the future, either," Bob put in. He had gotten to his feet and was restlessly pacing around the room. "Seems to be a directing intelligence of some kind at work here. Someone is trying to scare us out. That odor in the bedroom, Dad. The rest of us haven't noticed that. So it's you and Mom that are being worked on now because if you leave, the rest of us go, too. Then the house would be theirs again."

Dorothy, who had been listening thoughtfully, now spoke up. "I was worried and a little frightened," she admitted. "I pushed you into trying to get out of the lease. Now I'm beginning to get my dander up! I find I can take a lot of annoyance for seventy-two hundred dollars, plus the cost of moving and the effort of trying to find another place. Besides, we've worked hard on this house and should eventually have the opportunity to enjoy it!"

I could have cheered but I spoke quietly. "Well, we've all got to agree. Frankly, I can't afford to lose the money right now and I couldn't take the publicity of a court action for obvious reasons. But you're all members of this family and you each have a vote. We're in this together."

"I think it can be handled," said Hal decidedly. "It's only a matter of learning how to do it—and sticking it out until we do learn."

"I agree," said Bob enthusiastically.

Carrol was not to be outdone. "Me, too," he cried.

I looked at Dorothy. I would be away much of the time and she would be responsible for the welfare of the children in my absence. It would be up to her to overcome an instinctive fear of the unknown and keep things calm.

She looked back at me for several seconds and then shrugged in an attempt at nonchalance while a little smile tugged at her mouth.

"I've been doing some mental arithmetic," she said, "and I figure it won't be too bad. We have only one year, eleven months, one day and one night to go."

The conference broke up on that note of agreement. I turned out the lights, locked up, and followed the family upstairs to bed. As things turned out, it was an uneventful night. Maybe our antagonists, defeated in their attempts at intimidation, were regrouping their forces. We felt that a challenge had been issued and accepted and the next day Hal came home from the library laden with books by supposed experts on psychic phenomena.

"I've found out one thing," he announced at dinner the next night. "A lot of cases reported as being in the psychic activity category are eventually explained by natural causes. I don't think we've done enough investigating around here."

I agreed. I hadn't forgotten Brooks's reminder that our case would be a weak one in a court of law. "What do you have in mind?" I asked.

"I just feel that we haven't exhausted all possibilities and that some perverted mind may be at the bottom of these disturbances."

"There may be a secret entrance to this place—a secret tunnel. Someone in the area may have a private reason for wanting the premises empty," Bob cried out. "It could even be a dope smuggling headquarters or something!"

"Hardly that," I demurred. "Otherwise we wouldn't

be forced to stay here under the lease. But I think you're right and we'd better go to work."

And go to work we did. We made a thorough search of the mansion, inside and out. We tapped walls to find a hollow echo that would indicate a secret room or hallway. We paced over every foot of the grounds—even down by the creek—in search of an old, forgotten tunnel entrance to an underground passage.

As an added precaution, I secured the house so that entrance was impossible without the cooperation of someone inside. I put on new locks and added a hasp lock and a barrel bolt to every door. Both back entrances locked from the inside. There were bars across the library windows and the door leading to the outside yard from the library was locked and nailed shut with a twenty-pound spike. I also had a string of lights installed in the basement that could be turned on from the kitchen to brighten every room and crevice down there.

After securing the house, I took one more precaution. I bought Ching and Chang, two five-month-old chow puppies. These dogs are fierce, but highly intelligent and very easy to train and are phenomenally loyal to a family, especially the children. I felt safe with these two massive-jawed animals guarding the house.

If the owners of the nightly footsteps were clever and elusive enough to escape our detection, they certainly wouldn't get past Ching and Chang!

3

The Pact

Thank heaven the smells, sounds, and steps weren't a daily occurrence. Things would be quiet for a few days and then the footsteps would resume—either inside the house or out on the graveled path. We might sleep soundly for four or five nights and then be awakened by the offensive stench. When this happened we resignedly moved out of the area and waited for the odor to dissipate. We set up a daily routine and tried to live normally—if anything could be called "normal" under the circumstances. Hal and Bob were now in college and commuted daily in their own car except for the times they stayed over for some social or athletic event. I was home every minute that I could be.

There were even a few applicants for the positions we had listed with the local employment agency. We had always been particular about the type of help in our home and had never had any trouble in this respect. It soon became apparent, however, that we would have to take what help we could get. The first two hired were not from the area but could best be termed "drifters" if we were correctly interpreting their answers. However, they seemed respectable enough. They answered to the names of Mary and Clyde Simmons.

Clyde was tall, silent, nervous and thin. Mary was short, placid, voluble and fat. She was also the spokesman for the team. Her sentences invariably began with "Me and Clyde—we think—" or "Me and Clyde —we like—." This continued to the point where we privately referred to the man as "Simmons" and to his wife as "Me and Clyde." They both used so much snuff that the odor was noticeable—not only around their persons—but also when the door leading to the servants' quarters was opened.

They were both fair workers and we had no fault to find with them. Unfortunately, they complained about us. I came downstairs for the breakfast that Mary had prepared while Dorothy got a few more moments of needed rest. Simmons was already at the table and looked glum. He refused to respond to my cheerful greeting.

Me and Clyde spoke first. "Mr. Cameron, we're leavin' today."

I was shocked. "Leaving?" I echoed. "But why? You haven't been here long enough to decide if you really like us."

"I don't like being spied on—not in my own bed, I don't."

"Oh!" I replied lamely. So that was what it was! What could I say?

"Mary," I finally went on defensively. "No one here is spying on you. Neither Mrs. Cameron nor I would do such a thing! Your quarters are your own. We wouldn't think of bothering you there—not unless we had something important to say and knocked first—and were invited in!"

I said the wrong thing.

"You don't knock—and then disappear?" Her eyes narrowed speculatively.

"Of course not!" I answered stoutly.

She gave me a thoughtful look. "If neither you or the Missus is spying on us—if you don't knock and then go away before I can get to the door—then I don't even want to know *what* it is!"

I said nothing.

"Anyways, Mr. Cameron, Me and Clyde are leaving. We like the family fine but we don't exactly like this house. 'Sides, we have relatives in Tennessee. We're goin' to visit 'em."

Leave they did—almost immediately—in the old car that had brought them to our door in the first place.

"Now what?" I asked Dorothy rather helplessly.

She sighed. "At least I got the house cleaned properly and a pile of ironing done," she said. "We'll just have to try again."

During our first month in the house, I would rush home from work to check on Dorothy and the kids. When I found them safe and unharmed, I began to relax. Perhaps Bob was right. Nothing seemed about to physically injure us, in or around the house. I think my greatest contribution to the situation at this time was my insistence on keeping an objective, scientific attitude toward the phenomena we were experiencing. Dorothy cooperated with me in this, keeping us all calm in the wake of the midnight walks and unseen footsteps. She believed that someone, somewhere, was protecting the family. At times, though, we slipped up in our resolve to be always cool and collected. Carrol's ordeal was one of those times.

It was shortly after Me and Clyde and her spouse, Simmons, had left us that Dorothy and I found it necesssary to be away from the house one evening. We didn't worry about Carrol because his brothers were due back from an outing late that afternoon and nothing would bother our youngest son in the daytime. When we drove home that evening, however, we saw that the older boys' car was not parked in its usual place.

"Where have they all gone?" Dorothy wondered aloud. "It isn't like them to leave with all the lights on!" Janet and Michael had been left at the baby sitter's and were now in the car with us.

When we opened the front door we could see straight down the hall. There, sitting rigidly in a chair against the wall, was Carrol with a rifle across his knees. It was then that we realized that his brothers had not yet come home and he had been alone in the house for several hours.

Carrol surrendered the rifle to me without a word, but his lips were trembling.

"I'm sorry, son," I said contritely. "I didn't realize that you would be here alone. I thought your brothers would be with you. Otherwise—"

"Otherwise," Dorothy interrupted swiftly, "we would never have gone—no matter how important our business was!"

Carrol was shaken, but game. "Who said I was alone?" he countered with a pitiful attempt at a smile, as he told us what had happened.

Realizing that he was going to be by himself in the house after dark, he turned on all the lights, but that hadn't really been much comfort. He heard footsteps and was aware of a presence in the house. Finally, he went for the gun. Then he settled himself down to wait until someone—his brothers or his parents—arrived home.

In the midst of his fear and confusion, he heard the chows barking outside. There was a loud banging on the kitchen door.

"Anybody home?" a voice yelled. "Call off these damned dogs!"

Carrol wavered between a determination to ignore the noise and a feeling that he should be man enough to investigate. He heard the words and reminded himself that voices were something we had never heard from our unseen visitors. He decided to open the door, but kept the gun in his hand.

A man stood there in the twilight. He was dirty and disreputable looking and held a jug in his hand. It was difficult to say which of the two was more startled—Carrol, who had feared that he wouldn't be confronted by a real person—or the man, who certainly hadn't expected to be met by a boy and a rifle.

"What do you want?" Carrol demanded. He told us later that he wanted to be sure that this man spoke in a voice he could hear, so his own words had been loud and angry.

"I just w-wanted to f-fill my jug with water, sonny," the stranger gulped. "Is it all right?" He eyed the gun uncertainly and edged a few steps backward.

"It's all right," Carrol managed to mumble. "Come on in."

Under Carrol's watchful eye the man quickly filled his jug at the kitchen sink, still watching Carrol and the gun. Then he just as quickly went to the door.

"Thanks . . . thanks a lot, sonny," he said in a confused sort of way. At the door he paused.

"Can you really shoot that thing?" he asked.

"I can shoot it," replied Carrol grimly.

"But what—why—?"

Carrol realized that some sort of explanation was in order. People didn't usually answer a door with gun in hand.

"I'm sorry, sir," he said quietly. "I thought you might be a ghost."

"A ghost?" The man's voice went up a full octave. "Me?"

"I can see now that you aren't, of course," Carrol replied. "But we have them around here."

"Ghosts?" The man looked beyond Carrol into the hall. Then he half-ran from the house and tore around to the front drive, the jug wobbling in his hand.

Carrol relocked the back door. Then he went back to his position in the hall. Even though one interruption had proved to be entirely normal, he wasn't taking any chances. He didn't stop to think that an unseen entity would hardly have been intimidated by a gun. He remained tense and alert until he heard the sound of our car in the driveway and, a few seconds later, our voices in the hall. He was weak with relief at our arrival or he would probably have come rushing to meet us. As it was, his knees were trembling and he just sat there until I took the gun from him.

When Bob and Hal arrived a few moments later they were as upset as I was about Carrol's experience. They said they'd tried to phone to let us know they would be delayed, but there had been no answer.

"Where were you, anyway?" Hal asked Carrol crossly. I knew his irritation stemmed from his own worry and remorse.

"Out in the yard with the dogs, I guess. I didn't hear the phone."

"We just thought you'd all gone some place together," Bob said. "Otherwise, we'd never have stopped to eat on our way home."

After the two youngest children had been put to bed I decided it was time to call another family conference. Again we sat in the library and again I had their undivided attention.

"I think it's time we compared notes," I said. "I'm open to any new ideas or suggestions. Carrol just didn't imagine he heard those footsteps in the house and we're not going to insult him by suggesting that he did."

"Well, I've got one idea right now," Hal volunteered. "But if it was just floated to me, I'd like to know which side it's coming from."

I was curious. "Let's have it."

"Well, we hear them, don't we? We don't see them, but we hear them all right. Now why can't they hear us?"

"What makes you think they don't?" Bob asked. "They know when we're around. They know what room to go into when we're trying to sleep."

"They hear," Hal agreed, "or they sense us in some way. But they don't listen! Why don't we all try to get them to listen to us for a change?"

Dorothy's forehead puckered in concentration. "You mean have a meeting of the minds?"

"Sort of."

I thought over the suggestion. I could find nothing wrong with it—and, perhaps, a great deal to recommend it.

"Then I'll call this meeting to order," I announced. "We are here in the library. That, itself, seems to be important."

We had, by mutual consent, avoided the library which should have been the most pleasant room in the house. But once we had become settled in our new quarters, the library was the room that had troubled us the most. We were not comfortable while in it. It was in the library that our lady's footsteps were first heard and she seemed to spend a great deal of time there. The library door had opened by itself on numerous occasions. Finally it was placed off limits by unspoken agreement and we kept the door closed —when we could.

Now, seated in that room with only one small light burning, I felt it might be the proper thing to open the conference with prayer but I didn't know how to start. I was too self-conscious. The only words that came to mind at the moment were from the Grace before meals: "For what we are about to receive, O Lord, make us duly grateful." I decided that was hardly appropriate for this meeting. While not exactly tempting Providence, something less than a benevolent spirit might be stirred by those words.

We agreed to merely sit quietly until we felt a "presence" of some sort. I don't attribute it to our combined imaginations that this feeling wasn't long in coming. The boys moved restlessly. I felt that *something* was there and when I glanced over at Dorothy, she nodded her head slightly. Perhaps this *something* had been there all along. I started to talk.

"We know you are here. We don't know who you are or why you are here. We don't know, either, why you keep hanging around this place."

"We don't know who you are, but we do know that you don't seem to like us," Hal interrupted emphatically.

"And we don't like you much better," I agreed. "We know you'd like to get rid of us and we'd like equally as much to go. The trouble is that we can't leave. We're stuck here on a lease—and we have no place to go. So we are staying for a while longer. Is that understood?"

My words would have seemed completely idiotic to an outsider—but we were very much on the inside. I went on calmly. "We'd like to make an arrangement —or an agreement—with you. This is a sort of truce —a pact."

I fell silent for a moment. Somehow it seemed important that I choose the right words. I had to say just what was in my mind.

"We'll be here less than two years more if time means anything to you in your present state. But maybe you can remember what two years mean to us on a physical plane. During this time we'll keep any bargain we make with you. And now we'd like to draw up some boundary lines."

Again I hesitated. Again it didn't seem at all incongruous that I should be speaking to something I couldn't see, but could certainly sense.

Dorothy spoke for the first time. "The kitchen should be mine," she said. "It's all new, anyway, and not what you were used to."

I agreed. "None of you have been interested in the new kitchen and that should be Dorothy's domain. You seem to want us to stay out of the library here and, after tonight, we will stay out except to clean and dust once in a while—and that should please you regardless of where you are. You can have the entire third floor to yourselves. We don't need it or want it and I'm going to shut it off with plywood, anyway, because it will be too hard to heat this winter. I suppose you'll use the halls just as you always have, but try and be quiet about it."

"What about the outside?" Bob prompted.

I nodded. "As for the old coach house, you can have

that, too. I'm speaking to whoever uses it as head-quarters. We'll not interfere with you if you don't interfere with us. Is that agreed?"

There was complete silence in the room. I refused to give in to my own sneaking feeling that I might well be talking to empty air. I refused to accept the fact that I might be some sort of fool.

"I know there is a woman here," I went on. "I should say a lady because that's the way we have come to think of her. She has good manners as a rule. She doesn't throw things around or make noise. I feel that she is curious about the people in this house, but that is her privilege. Otherwise, she seems to mind her own business—whatever that might be. I also presume that she was once mistress of this house and doesn't want to leave it. Well, she doesn't have to leave it. We will keep her house clean and attractive, but we'd like to be treated as her guests until we can leave."

I rose to my feet. "I am sure the lady has nothing to do with the bad odor in our bedroom at times. This must be the man. It isn't going to push us out because, as I have explained, we have no other place to go. I still think, however, that this is the lady's house and she can help control things."

I motioned to the family and they rose quietly and started for the hall as I concluded. "That's all for now. We are leaving the library to you. We wish you nothing but the best. Goodnight!"

After we left the library there was no idle conversation. We all felt that somehow my words had been heard. All of us were very quiet and reflective. I turned off the light and closed the door firmly behind me. Then we went upstairs to bed.

"I suppose I should feel like an idiot of sorts," Dorothy remarked as she sat in front of her dressing table. "But somehow I don't. These people have become very real to me and I think this conversation was long overdue. Even though," she added as an afterthought, "it appeared to be a one-sided talk."

We don't know if anyone but the family listened to my speech. At least it gave us all an emotional boost. We felt that we had cleared the air in some inexplicable way. Perhaps because we really felt that to be true, we were less disturbed from that time on.

The odor in our bedroom continued in spasmodic fashion for the rest of our time there, but we took it in stride. Sometimes we even admitted, rather sheepishly perhaps, that when we heard footsteps in the hall we were inclined to step courteously aside and let them pass.

There was only one drawback to this inner assurance and regained confidence. Other people, unfortunately, couldn't share it.

4
Things That Go
Bump in the Night

Our first visit from relatives was heralded by a letter from my sister Elda Clare Tillman who lived with her husband, Burchell, on a cattle ranch in New Mexico. We had sent her a picture of the house and she had immediately decided that a vacation was in order. She soon wrote:

I can't wait to see your mansion. It intrigues me no end. I, also, can't wait to see some of my favorite people that I've missed very much and I'm ready for a shopping trip to New York with Dorothy to help me pick out hats. Will bring Lana and Larry and will notify you of our intended arrival just as soon as my plans at this end are completed which won't take long.

Much love,
Elda Clare

My sister had been active in politics and club work, had a beautiful singing voice and was much in demand to perform at important functions. She was also a devoted mother. We always enjoyed Elda Clare; tall and slim, with a smile for everyone. She was talented, level-headed, and about as normal as a person could be. Larry was eight and just the right age to play with Carrol, who was missing youthful companionship. Lana was Janet's age and the two had always loved each other. This was a perfect family with whom to initiate our entertaining in our new home. If we were without help during her visit—and we were in that condition more often than not—she would pitch in with the work. But there was a problem. How much should we tell her about the house being haunted?

"I rather think she should be warned—at least a little," said Dorothy thoughtfully. "Remember the shock that poor little Joe got!"

"And how do you warn just a little?" I demanded. "It has to be all or nothing. Besides," I added with a grin, "I don't see Elda Clare camping on the lawn!"

Joe was a friend of Carrol's from our Portland days who had visited for a short time. The boys had decided to "rough it." They set up a tent on the front lawn and had two dogs, a gun, and a flashlight to bolster their courage. It was a moonlit night and everything went well until the dogs started to bark. Then, to Carrol's uneasiness, the dogs crept closer to him, their barks changing to frightened whimpers. Heavy footsteps were heard on the gravel. They came to the front drive. Carrol turned on his flashlight but no one was there. The steps passed them, went around to the kitchen entrance and stopped. (This was the only time to my knowledge they hadn't stopped at the front door.) Boys and dogs fled to the house and that ended their camping venture.

"Gee, Mr. Cameron," Joe said. "The guy was so close I could have untied his shoelaces—but I didn't see any shoes!"

"Did the kitchen door open?" I asked curiously.

Carrol shook his head. "It didn't have to," he replied somberly.

Joe's eyes were wide with fear. It was probably the first time that anything had happened an adult couldn't explain away. It must have been a difficult experience for the boy. It was even a harder one for Carrol as Joe would be going home in a day or two where such things didn't happen. Carrol would have to continue living in the house and face the unknown along with the rest of his family. Carrol later said this was the first time he ran *into* the house for safety!

As we continued to discuss the pros and cons of a complete confession to Elda Clare, Bob impishly embarked on an impromptu parody on Hamlet.

> "To tell, or not to tell, that is the question.
> Whether 'tis nobler for their minds to suffer
> The slings and arrows of . . . of . . ."

Here Bob floundered, but Hal caught the ball.

> "Of outrageous forces, or to forewarn them of our many troubles,
> And, in compassion, tell them."

Although we laughed together at the joint declamation, we were still uncertain about a course of action.

"I don't know how she'd take it," I admitted truthfully. "In the first place I doubt if she'd believe a word. Then, if she should ridicule the idea of disembodied entities around, they just might get angry enough to shake her up!"

"And us along with her," Bob pointed out. "Sometimes I feel they are capable of causing a lot more trouble than they already have."

"We'll just keep quiet and play it by ear," I finally decided.

Elda Clare arrived on schedule. She loved the whole place—from the mansion with its spacious rooms and grand atmosphere to the grounds, the coach house, maple tree and summerhouse. She was so enthused that we looked around with new eyes and were happier about the mansion than we had been for some time.

My sister had arrived with plenty of money for incidental expenses and for the New York shopping spree she had mentioned in her letter. This was in the "old" days when a new hat usually answered any woman's problem from a spell of blues to a fit of temper. I was amused at her excited anticipation, but could understand it. Although Dorothy had given no indication of needing a new hat to improve her disposition, I felt that the outing to New York would do her good. The two days following Elda Clare's arrival had been uneventful as far as ghostly visitations were concerned and we were more relaxed.

Dorothy was able to get a baby sitter for a few hours, so they drove to the airport, parked the car, and flew to New York which was only minutes away by air from Philadelphia. There they spent a happy morning. They bought the hats first and left the remainder of the shopping until after a very swank luncheon which they enjoyed tremendously.

After lunch Elda Clare decided that she wanted a

paper to use as a shopping guide and laid her purse down for a moment while she selected one. This is a mistake in any city, but particularly in New York. When she turned around, paper in hand, her purse had disappeared.

Filled with consternation, the two of them searched everywhere and asked questions of bystanders—all to no avail. The purse was gone. Elda Clare was upset because personal cards and identification were in the purse, together with checkbook and four hundred dollars in cash. Fortunately, Dorothy had put the return plane tickets in her own purse and still had some money left. But such a damper had been put on the shopping expedition that they decided to return home.

That night Elda Clare phoned Burchell, telling him about the theft and asking that he forward more money. He told her not to let the incident spoil her trip and promised to wire extra money the next day. While talking to him, she laid her cigarettes on the hall table which was located very near the library door. I noticed them there before I went to bed, but only gave them a cursory glance.

The next morning was Sunday and breakfast was later than usual. I hadn't had too much chance to talk with my sister and looked forward to a leisurely visit. However, when she came to the table, I noticed that she looked tired and responded to our greetings in a bemused fashion. Suddenly I felt a stir of apprehension. I didn't feel that her distraught appearance could be attributed to the loss of money that Burchell could well afford to replace.

"What's the matter?" I asked. "Didn't you sleep well?"

"No," she replied shortly.

I went on. "The kids okay?"

I knew the question was superfluous as Larry had already bounded down the stairs, consumed an amazing amount of ham and eggs, and was out in the yard with Carrol and the dogs. Lana and Janet were still asleep upstairs.

As she still remained silent, I kept on. "Burchell wasn't too upset about your losing that money, was he?"

"No," she replied slowly. "It isn't Burchell and it isn't the children. It's me!" Then she added in a rush, "Harold, I've got something to tell you—and you aren't going to believe a word!"

I sighed. "Try me," I suggested simply.

"Well—there's something wrong with this house. Something is here that doesn't belong here—that's what!" she blurted out.

"You might as well tell us about it." I hoped I didn't sound as resigned as I felt. Dorothy, who had been feeding cereal to Michael, held her spoon in midair.

"Well—last night I was still so annoyed at being 'took' like a country hick that I couldn't get to sleep." She suddenly slapped her hand down on the table. "This would never have happened in New Mexico. People there don't steal like that!"

I grinned. "They wouldn't steal a purse, but I've known cattle to vanish into thin air. But go on!"

She took a deep breath. "I wanted a cigarette but I had left them on the telephone table in the hall. I didn't want to wake Larry or disturb the rest of you so I didn't turn on the lights. I knew the layout of the house. I just went down the stairs and straight down the hall to the table. I had the feeling that the library door was open and you said you always kept it closed,

but I didn't think about it until later. I was fumbling
for the cigarettes and finally found them and—well—
I heard someone there in the hall. The footsteps came
across to where I stood."

"So?"

"I knew it wasn't any of you or you would have
answered when I asked who it was. But somebody
just walked over to me and stood there in the dark. It
was a woman, I'm sure. She had slippers on her feet.
Harold, she was so close that I could hear her breathing!"

I smiled a little. "No, you didn't, sis. You didn't hear
this one breathing. What did you do then?"

"Do?" she echoed shrilly. "I ran—that's what I did.
I ran up those stairs in the dark, locked the bedroom
door and climbed into bed with Larry! I stayed there
all night with my face to the wall and head covered.
That's what I did! I thought morning would never
come!"

Dorothy absently guided the spoon to Michael's
waiting mouth as I was silent for a moment or two,
wondering where to start. Elda Clare evidently mis-
interpreted my attitude for one of disbelief for she
burst out indignantly, "Don't you dare say it was just
my imagination! It really happened—and nothing
like that ever happened to me before in my whole
life!"

I sighed again. "I think it's time we had a little
talk," I told her.

"But do you believe me?" she demanded.

"Yes, I believe you. Listen to me, now!" So I talked
and she listened—incredulously at first and then with
mounting indignation.

"Why didn't you warn me?" she demanded when I
had finished. "Why did you let me walk right into it?"

I was a little uncomfortable. Come to think of it, that was my usual state of mind when I was forced to explain about our unseen residents.

"Well, honey, if you hadn't come down in the night and hadn't been so close to the library, you might never have known anything about it," I told her. "Sometimes we hear this woman—sometimes we don't. Besides, would you have believed me before you experienced it for yourself?"

She was honest. "I probably would have thought you had rocks in your head," she finally admitted. Then her customary smile broke through. "Now that I know the truth, I feel better. At least I'm not the only one with rocks!"

"You have plenty of company," I assured her and there was a relieved smile on Dorothy's face.

"I think I'm hungry," Elda Clare announced. "You and Dorothy act so matter of fact about this that it must be an ordinary occurrence. How about telling me more while I eat breakfast and before the girls come down?"

So I told about the visitations in our bedrooms, the frightened servants, the footsteps on the gravel when Joe and Carrol were camping out and the whimpering dogs. I wouldn't have blamed her when I finished the recital if she had cut her visit short. However, the situation appealed to her sense of adventure. She joined in our ritual of tapping walls and checking doors and windows. She listened avidly while we gathered around the kitchen table at night and told of our other experiences.

During one of these sessions Elda Clare happened to have her eyes on the basement door and stopped suddenly in the middle of a lively recital of an experience she had undergone with a half-broken pony.

She stared incredulously and then indicated what had caught her attention by wordlessly pointing her finger in that direction. We turned in our chairs and saw that the doorknob of the basement door was turning slowly back and forth. The door was locked and further secured by a bolt on the kitchen side.

Gesturing for silence, I found two flashlights to help with illumination in the shadowy basement as the bright new lights had not, as yet, been installed. Then I moved quickly to the door, unbolted it, and flung it open. No one could be seen by the beam from the flashlights or by the old globe hanging from the ceiling when I finally pulled the string. We went on down the stairs, keeping close together for moral support and made a thorough search of the entire premises. There was no one there.

Somewhat subdued, we went back upstairs and relocked the door, agreeing to make another search in the comfortable light of day.

"But just look at those windows, Harold," Elda Clare said soberly when we again gathered in the basement the next morning. "They all have iron bars across them that are set in cement. No one could get in that way. That only leaves the coal chute."

"And that's way up at outside ground level," I pointed out. "You'd need a ladder to reach it from this basement floor. Besides, it has a heavy iron grating over it and that is secured."

"No one could have escaped, anyway," Hal observed. "It was only a matter of seconds until we had that door open and went down with flashlights."

Elda Clare shivered. "It's certainly uncanny," she admitted. "Even now if anyone should ask me if I believed in ghosts, I'd probably say I didn't. But I'm afraid that would be a mechanical response due to my former mental conditioning. But, Harold, what other explanation is there for these crazy happenings?"

"I promise you one thing," I said grimly. "I'm going to have such bright lights installed down here that a half-blind person could thread a needle in every corner! I've already ordered the installation of more lights, but they just haven't gotten around to it yet. Now I'm going to order twice as many units and tell them to get moving on it!"

The very next day I carried out my promise and contacted the electrician.

Elda Clare and the kids finished their vacation with us and we enjoyed every moment of it. However, she didn't wander about the house at night, she kept her bedroom door locked, and stayed away from the library even in the daytime. She and Dorothy went back to New York and completed their interrupted shopping trip. Eventually she returned to New Mexico—somewhat wiser, but none the worse for her experiences. In a letter she wrote us later on, she stated:

The memory and *feel* of the house—the grounds—that high rock fence—the barking of dogs in the mist-filled mornings—all these and a few other important and unexplainable things—will live in vivid recollection as long as I have breath!

My sister-in-law, Ernestine, reacted much differently when she came to visit. Ernestine was attractive enough but highly temperamental. She was auburn-haired, green-eyed, nervously thin and excitable. She was, also, quite often irritable and almost psychotic, for life had turned sour with Ernestine. She and my brother had separated and she was inclined to brood over her wrongs, both real and imagined. However, she felt that a visit with us in our new home would do her good and help to restore what she termed her "equilibrium"—not realizing how little she had of that to begin with.

I know I should have explained the situation of the house immediately—or asked her to postpone her visit for the time being. But again, I didn't know what to count on. Perhaps there would be ghostly manifestations—perhaps not. We were going to have to come to terms with this uncertainty during the balance of our stay in that house, so I agreed that Ernestine could come, but I also intended to alert her to certain strange possibilities. However, she arrived tired and nervous and, after a quick tour of the house, wanted to go to bed early. It didn't seem the right time to tell her to simply ignore the footsteps in her room or the unexplained opening of doors. I was to wish later on that I had warned her.

We were all asleep when the crash sounded. It came from downstairs with such force that I felt there had been an explosion. The three boys were out of bed instantly. They ran for our bedroom. I was already out of bed and getting into my slippers. I didn't bother looking for a robe.

"Dad!" Hal shouted from the doorway. "I think the furnace blew up!"

Dorothy had streaked into the nursery to see if the babies were all right and found them undisturbed. She came back and hurriedly slipped into a robe. "Where was the noise?" she asked.

"I think it was in the library," I replied, leading the way down the hall. "It sounded just beneath us."

At that moment Ernestine raced down the hall and threw herself into my arms. She was sobbing and wild-eyed, shaking all over.

"Someone tried to kill me!" she screamed.

I grasped her shoulders and tried to shake the

mounting hysterics out of her. "What happened? Calm down! You're all right now!"

"Th-the l-library," she stuttered, pointing toward the stairs. "Th-there in the l-library!"

"Her library," Hal muttered.

I ignored him. "Come on!" I commanded the boys. "It sounded as if the entire cornice of the fireplace gave way!"

Ernestine still held me with a death-like grip. I transferred her to Dorothy's arms. "You go back in the bedroom with Dorothy!" I ordered. "We'll investigate!"

We raced to the library where I switched on the lights. I had expected a room in shambles. It was in perfect order with Ernestine's book lying on the floor. I stared at the boys who were as mystified as I. We went back upstairs where Dorothy had succeeded in quieting Ernestine for the moment.

"What were you doing in the library at this time of night?" I asked.

She swallowed convulsively. "R-reading, of course. I couldn't sleep . . . I kept thinking about things . . . so I decided to go downstairs and read until I was sleepy. I must have dozed off and then . . ." her voice rose hysterically, "then this thing . . . this terrible thing crashed right beside my head and hit the floor. I—I could have been killed, I tell you!"

"Well, you weren't," I replied, not unkindly. "But we all heard the noise, so it wasn't your imagination."

"Imagination!" she screeched. "I'm attacked in your home and you speak of imagination!"

"But you could have had a bad nightmare," I pointed out reasonably. "People do and they seem very real. Now you stay here again with Dorothy while the boys and I look around some more."

"Do you think it was the furnace, Dad?" Hal asked, looking around.

"Your guess is as good as mine," I told him. "I thought the noise came from the library, myself. You know it's just below our bedroom. But let's have a look at that furnace."

The basement door was locked and bolted. I unlocked it and turned on the lights. We made a thorough examination of the whole basement, including the furnace room. We could find nothing wrong, so we went back upstairs where Ernestine filled in more of the details. She was more in control now, but still shaking.

"I fell asleep down there, like I said. Then there was this awful crash. I rolled right over the back of the divan and across the table. Then I ran. What was it? What on earth . . . ?"

"Maybe someone was dynamiting," Bob suggested rather weakly. I mentally thanked him for not replying that it probably had been nothing on earth.

"Dynamite? At this time of night? Don't be silly," Ernestine snapped.

"We'll talk about it in the morning and look around outside. Right now you are going to take some aspirin and go back to bed. And you stay there!"

"Don't worry about that," she sniffed.

Something had been nagging at my mind for several moments and suddenly I knew what it was. I remembered how dark and still the library had been when we went down to investigate.

"Ernestine," I questioned when we had tucked her in for the rest of the night. "You said you were reading and just dozed off?"

She nodded, swallowing the aspirin that Dorothy had handed her with a glass of water. "That's right."

"But if you were so scared that you just rolled over the back of the sofa, how did you take the time to turn off the light you were reading by?"

She looked bewildered. "I never touched that light! I told you—I just ran!" It took a full minute for the significance of my question to sink in. Then she gasped, "Harold, was that library dark?"

I nodded without speaking.

She gave her head a little shake as though trying to clear it. "Then someone was in the house," she said, horrified. "Who was with me in that library? Who turned off the light?"

"We'll reason things out in the morning, Ernestine. Let's try and get some sleep now."

Not that I thought she'd take my advice, of course. After I closed her door, she got out of bed and slid the bolt. I wondered a little grimly if locking that door was going to do any good. I knew that another visit to her room could send her over the brink.

"What time is it?" I asked Dorothy when we were back in bed.

"Past two o'clock," she sighed.

I groaned aloud. "I'm not sleepy after this commotion. I'll be in great shape for that Washington conference tomorrow."

"Roll over and I'll rub your back," she offered. I relaxed to the soothing stroke of her fingers on my spine. She asked only one question. "Harold, can you figure it out?"

"Nope. I'm completely in the dark about it. If invisible entities can generate noises like that, this whole planet should be in an uproar."

"It is a lot of the time," she reminded me. "And I've been thinking about Ernestine's book. It did fall from her lap. Maybe our lady couldn't initiate the noise herself, but she could amplify and expand the sound made when the book hit the floor."

I thought a moment. "I'll buy that," I said at last. "Mainly because I can't come up with any other alternative at the moment. What bothers me is the light being turned off."

"That isn't as surprising as the noise," she said. "I've read that electric switches are more or less easy for entities to handle. Anyway, it seems to me like a mother who spanked a child and sent her up to bed —and then turned off the light."

The situation was anything but funny. Still, I chuckled a little. Somehow that picture was less terrifying than other things which had crossed my mind. "Let's get some sleep," I suggested.

I had thought that Ernestine would spend the day in bed, letting Dorothy wait on her. Evidently she wanted to be around people because she joined us at breakfast, looking pale and worried. We were forced to explain the situation in the house and advised her to stay out of the library from then on.

Ernestine listened to my recital without once interrupting. Then she said stonily, "I wouldn't have believed any of this before. Now I do. I not only believe it, but I think you are all in danger every minute you're in this house. As for me, I'm going straight home. At least I'm safe there!"

And go home she did, leaving us apologetic, frustrated and helpless.

"I guess it was all our fault in a way," Dorothy sighed that night at dinner. "We really didn't mean to —but the pact was broken."

"Well, it proves one thing at least," Hal replied, staring down at his plate with a thoughtful expression.

"What?" Dorothy asked.

"Someone must have listened that night in the library, after all."

"Do you think they will hold it against us?" asked Bob rather apprehensively.

I shook my head. "I don't think so. If our lady is as smart as she seems to be, she will have detected the fact that it was a stranger who invaded her domain—not one of us."

Ernestine's experience taught us another lesson. When my mother and dad were on their way from New Mexico for a visit, I phoned Elda Clare and asked if she had confided in them regarding her experiences in the house. She had not.

"I didn't tell them a word, Harold. You know them as well as I do. They simply wouldn't have believed me—so I thought it best to let well enough alone."

However, the first night they were with us, we explained the situation.

My dad had been a pastor in Dodge City in Kansas, in Hutchinson and in Kansas City. He was loved and respected. Mother was a person in her own right and had led an interesting life—as well as a practical and respectable one. In addition to being a pastor's wife with all the attendant extracurricular activities, she had served as matron and assistant superintendent of the Missouri Penitentiary for Women. In that capacity she "sat" with Bonnie Brown Headly, a convicted murderer, during her last thirty days on earth. Mother was efficient, mentally alert, and at the age of eighty-one, was to publish a book entitled *Looking Through the Windows*. She was compassionate and practical and her emotions were always under control. After the now-familiar recital, my parents stared at me with mixed emotions.

Dad shook his head solemnly. "This has to be a case of mass-hallucination," he said at last. "I'm a little surprised at you, Harold. But I suppose it is more or less natural to be overly imaginative in an old place like this."

I was slightly nettled. "What do you mean? I've been in a lot of old places before. This is something entirely different."

"But you haven't lived in those old places," he pointed out. "This house has an entirely different atmosphere."

"I grant you that," I retorted. "But what created this atmosphere in the first place?"

He was thinking up an answer to that when I looked over at my mother. She had the same expression on her face that she wore when, in my boyhood, she'd felt it necessary to wash my mouth out with soap.

"Tsch, tsch, Harold," she said reprovingly.

I shrugged in resignation. Elda Clare had been right. "Well, I just thought I'd tell you how things are around here," I said weakly.

Dorothy had remained silent through my recital and she now ushered my parents up to their room. When she came back I lifted an eyebrow in silent interrogation. She only shook her head.

"They wouldn't even discuss it," she replied. "Maybe things will go all right. We can only hope for the best."

There were no footsteps to their room during their visit, nor did the odor bother them. There was one incident, which seemed out of character, but still unbelievable.

We had a heavy snowfall the second day they were with us and that night we all stood at the window admiring the beauty of the unblemished white landscape. The next morning Mother came down to breakfast absolutely beaming.

"You dear children," she smiled. "What a sweet thing to do!"

"What do you mean?" Dorothy asked.

"That lovely vase of flowers! How did you find such beautiful ones at this time of year? They are a perfect spring bouquet." She stopped then and looked puzzled. "Where did you get them? Did you have them flown in just for me? Were they delivered during the night?"

Dorothy and I exchanged bewildered glances.

"We had nothing to do with it," I disclaimed. Mother looked over at Hal and Bob who shook their heads, equally mystified. We trooped up the stairs after her to see the flower arrangement that had so pleased her. There was a flower-filled vase on her dresser and it was as lovely as she had described.

Dorothy fingered the fluted vase and I suddenly remembered where I had last seen it. It had been on the dressing table in the master bathroom which was just across the hall from our bedroom, but quite a distance down the hall from the suite we had assigned to my parents.

"Isn't that your vase?" I asked Dorothy.

"It certainly is! I keep it in the bathroom to hold my imported soaps. It's been empty for a week now."

Mother was perplexed. "Then it was taken—really taken—from your bathroom, filled with flowers and brought to my room?" she demanded incredulously.

"It was," I replied emphatically. "And none of us did it!"

Dorothy smiled. "Congratulations, Mother dear," she

said. "You have passed inspection. You must have met with the unqualified approval of the unseen lady who is the real mistress of this house."

Mother's eyes were bulging. As she continued to be speechless, I drew her to the window. "Look down there," I urged. "There isn't a tire track or a footprint in that drive. How could we have had flowers delivered without a vehicle leaving a trace in the snow? Just to satisfy you, Dad and I will go down and look for tracks. We always try to find a logical explanation when things out of the ordinary happen, but so far we've found none. Nothing like *this* ever happened before!"

"But Harold," she protested in a small voice. "It can't have happened the way you think."

"What else?" I asked gently. "I'll bet you anything that we won't find a mark on that snow."

Mother recovered somewhat. "I am not a betting woman," she reminded me with a faint smile.

"Besides," I went on. "Where would we have gotten spring flowers? You asked that yourself."

Mother was finally shaken. She put both hands to her face. "Oh, Daddy," she wailed. "We weren't alone in our room last night!"

After we had thoroughly checked the grounds, leaving clear tracks in the snow wherever we went, even my orthodox father was convinced that we had been telling the truth. Something had happened for which he had no explanation. He was thoughtful and sober. No longer did he look askance at us if we happened to mention our lady. I didn't hear any more about mass hallucinations, either.

Whether or not my parents ever heard footsteps during the rest of their visit I do not know. If they did, they certainly kept quiet. Our ghost was something they preferred not to discuss. But when I told them we were having a little trouble getting qualified, permanent help and offered what I thought was a good proposition, we didn't see eye to eye.

"Look, Dad," I said persuasively. "We can't keep servants. I'll pay you a good salary, plus board, if you and Mother will stay and help out for the balance of our lease. The grounds are a full-time job and you understand flowers and shrubs. Mother could help Dorothy with the children and the light housework and . . ." I broke off at the expression on my mother's face.

"Harold," she said firmly. "We would really like to help you out, but I wouldn't live in this house for any amount of money."

Perhaps my mother had heard footsteps in the night, after all.

At the end of their visit, I saw them off on the plane. Then I came back home and went into the library. I made a quiet bid for attention.

"I want to thank you," I said to our unseen lady, "for the lovely thing you did for my mother. I feel that it could have been a sort of apology for scaring poor Ernestine half out of her wits. But this was a gracious gesture—those lovely flowers were the sort of gift that a real lady would make. If it was also an apology, I accept it—with thanks."

Then I turned on my heel and went out, closing the door firmly behind me. After all, I told myself, our lady deserved her privacy.

5

The Passing Parade

News of our haunted house leaked out at the office. It was all my fault. I had asked many people if they had ever heard of poltergeists or ghosts in some of the old places in Philadelphia and was instantly hit with a barrage of ghost stories. At one time I would have scoffed, but now I was much more tolerant. Sometimes I even told of some of our own happenings in the old mansion, hoping to get a fresh viewpoint or a new opinion.

There were seventeen women in the credit department and they were all thrilled at my stories. Most of them asked me for an invitation to visit our home.

"It isn't that I really believe in ghosts," Mary, a bookkeeper, confided. "But it all sounds so interesting that I'd love to come down. Do you think your wife would mind? I'd even do the dishes!" This seemed like such a concession on her part that I wondered if she ever did them in her own home. I avoided extending invitations until the staff ganged up on me.

"What's the matter, Mr. Cameron?" Ida asked. "Haven't you been leveling with us? Don't you want other witnesses?"

I had reached the point where I didn't mind other witnesses but I remembered Ernestine's reaction and I didn't want any more hysterical females on my hands. I finally agreed that a few could come out on weekends if they would come two at a time and share the same bedroom. What followed was the usual pattern. Sometimes sober-faced girls admitted that footsteps in a dark room weren't as entertaining as they had anticipated. At other times our unseen habitants simply ignored the whole situation. However, we always refused to let our guests into the library.

One day when we were once again without household help, I told Dorothy that a couple of the women would be arriving early Saturday afternoon.

She sighed. "They are very nice and even help a little with the work," she admitted. "But if you charged admission, it might also help with the food bills."

"I don't think I can do that," I replied. "When you charge admission to a show, you have to guarantee a performance."

She laughed a little. "I know that. I really should be grateful when the stage is dark—grateful for small favors." Suddenly she became very serious. "Harold, I really don't like referring to these phenomena as a show. I'm not too easy in my mind when you do it. Whatever takes place around here isn't funny—not to our unseen entities, anyway. I have the feeling there is a tragic cloud hanging over the premises. I don't think we should laugh or make light of it. Something must have happened long ago that left a very vivid psychic impression here—maybe something pretty terrible. Maybe, too, someone is really earthbound and in misery. We wouldn't have this same attitude if some of our visible friends happened to be in trouble."

I looked at her in surprise. "I didn't know you felt that way, too," I said. "It also occurs to me that we have changed a great deal since we moved into the mansion. Such a thing would never have entered our minds before we started reading up on psychic phenomena. From now on I'll discourage any visits from thrill seekers."

"Our lady has become very real to me," Dorothy once confessed. "I'm getting used to having her around. Besides, she's less trouble than some people I know."

I agreed wholeheartedly. I had been experiencing unforeseen difficulties for a month or so. Not only was I having trouble with unseen spirits at home, I had my hands full with very real entities at the office. Along with the day-to-day difficulties of conducting any kind of business, I had to deal with "the way things are done in Philadelphia." One incident involved a monthly payment to be made to a "highway superintendent" to insure space for a loading zone for our trucks.

The other incident was an even more serious—and frightening—attempt at extortion. A disgruntled customer wanted to return some merchandise and get a refund. The merchandise was not damaged—he was simply tired of it—"and needed the money." We refused to return his money. He left the office, muttering and glaring. Shortly after, a letter arrived at my office.

Mr. Cameron:

We've investigated you and know that you can pay. We want $15,780 in unmarked bills—and we want it soon so get it together and we'll contact you again. If you go to the police we are going to blow up your whole office with everybody in it—and take care of your family too.

I disregarded his warning. This, after all, was a clear and present danger, not ghostly footfalls on the path or in the library. The police seemed bored and unwilling to investigate. I called the FBI. They agreed to work on the case. I told them about the dissatisfied client. The FBI only succeeded in letting the man know that the authorities were after him.

I was livid! Now that my extortionist knew I had made contact with law enforcement agencies, he would probably carry out the rest of his threats. I tried the police again who were unwilling to enter the case which the FBI had apparently fumbled.

Finally, I went to the top. The mayor of Philadelphia listened attentively to my story. Protection was assigned to my home and office on a twenty-four-hour basis until the perpetrator—the same irate refund demander—was caught.

Reflecting on these incidents, I could only nod and tell Dorothy that, indeed, she was right. Sometimes an unseen presence could be easier to deal with—and far less threatening—than that which was perfectly visible!

Although we had finally come to terms with our ghostly situation, we all knew that it would be illogical to expect others to come to a similar acceptance. This was certainly true when it came to household help.

I hadn't exaggerated when I told my dad that we had trouble keeping servants. They lasted such a short time that I can't even recall all names and faces— even though I have a good memory. I became a regular visitor at the employment agency. In a very short time, I became an unwelcome one. There was no money to be made from the Camerons.

"What kind of a place are you running out there?" the agency manager finally asked irately. "It's hard to get people to even apply and, according to the grapevine, if they do try it, they'll be sorry."

I replied with what dignity I could muster that we had a nice home, got along very well with all our help, and were never unreasonable in our demands upon them in the matter of work. Naturally, I couldn't mention ghosts.

"That isn't exactly what I meant," the man replied. "Anyway, we've gone through the list. We don't have a soul for you right now."

Something told me that he wouldn't have a soul for us in the near future, either, so I went to another agency.

Although we preferred a husband and wife combination we settled on singles again. We hired Samantha as housekeeper and Ernie for the outside work. They had rooms in the servants' quarters and because their doors did not open into the upstairs hall, I felt there was no reason why they should be disturbed by unusual noises.

Samantha fed Ernie in the kitchen while the family ate in the dining room. They both seemed capable enough. After two weeks went by without apparent trouble, we began to hope that they would stay. It was futile. One day after a serious huddle, they both quit at the same time.

I tried to pin them down. "Just why do you want to leave?" I demanded.

"I got my reasons," Samantha said stubbornly and refused to discuss the matter any further.

"We just don't like certain things," Ernie answered evasively and clammed up when I tried further interrogation. They had already packed their belongings before announcing their joint decision to leave immediately. That night Dorothy again cooked dinner by herself.

I do remember Ellen. I liked her immensely. She stayed three weeks. She seemed placid and hardworking and was cheerful most of the time. It was pleasant to come down to breakfast in the morning and be greeted by her wide grin. However, this was before she decided to do some ironing in the dining room.

Humming to herself, she heard someone come in the door behind her and assumed that it was Dorothy who stood close at her shoulder and was evidently scrutinizing her ironing technique. She chatted happily to her mistress for a few minutes and then it occurred to her that Dorothy was unusually silent and hadn't answered her at all. She looked around. There was no one in the room but herself.

"Mrs. Cameron?" she called tentatively.

There was no answer. Ellen stood in petrified silence. She had heard the door open and had heard footsteps. She had felt a person stand very near and hadn't heard that person leave. She dropped the iron and went screeching through the house in search of Dorothy who had been upstairs for the last half-hour giving Michael his bath.

"Mrs. Cameron!" Ellen gasped. "Who's downstairs in the dining room?"

Dorothy recognized another crisis. She put Michael

down in his crib and handed him a bottle of orange juice.

"Come on, Ellen," she said resignedly. "I want to talk to you."

Downstairs Dorothy retrieved the iron and noted that the room was empty and the library door closed. Then she took Ellen into the kitchen and poured two cups of coffee. Feeling that she had established a good rapport, she sat down opposite Ellen at the breakfast table and began to explain about old houses.

"Sometimes certain things happen in old houses that are hard to understand, Ellen. The mansion is one of those places. You are perfectly safe here and you must just ignore certain things that happen—just as the rest of us do. No one has ever been hurt. We all love you very much and want you to be happy with us."

Her effort failed miserably.

"I'm sorry, Mrs. Cameron," Ellen said firmly as she pushed her untouched coffee away. "I'm quittin' right now. I like you and the mister fine and the work isn't that hard . . . but those certain things you talk about will just have to happen here without me!"

And that was that!

We finally started in on agencies in Philadelphia and after a while there was no one "suitable" on their lists, either. Our reputation—or the mansion's reputation to be exact—seemed to go before us but it did nothing to brighten our path. The answers given by servants to repeated inquiries were always the same and usually evasive. Yes, they liked Mr. and Mrs. Cameron just fine. No, the children weren't any trouble. But they just didn't think the house was "right."

About this time there was to be a Fourth of July

parade in Wynne. The boys were doing dishes so Dorothy could get Janet and Michael down at a proper hour.

"You know," Bob observed. "We don't have to go to town to see a parade. All we have to do is to stand here and watch our own—the parade of servants coming and going."

Hal agreed. "It's like an army. They march in right smart but they sure break ranks when they leave. You'd think this house was a bridge."

I had come into the kitchen in time to hear this exchange. "Maybe it is," I put in thoughtfully, "a bridge between two worlds."

I really meant that. I was convinced that there was another level of consciousness or activity of some kind that occupied the same space we did and even penetrated it. Certainly there was an interplay of some sort; an unexplained juxtaposition between entities in physical bodies and those in astral form. Why it was particularly noticeable in our location, I simply did not know.

I was finally driven to try a different approach. There was a handsome, strong young man at the warehouse who had just left the Marines. He was newly married and I knew the generous salary I was prepared to offer him would be attractive and probably needed. I decided to level with him.

"Look, Sam!" I said earnestly. "You're an ex-Marine and you aren't afraid of anything on earth. You can't be scared by old wives' tales. We have been living in our house for several months now and we don't pay any attention to odd noises and creakings and things like that."

Sam looked interested and I went on persuasively. "I've got a four-year-old daughter. Nothing has ever frightened her. Certainly if a child can live happily in that house, you and Margo can. You're a grown man of proven intelligence. You even got medals for bravery. How about you and Margo taking on this job for me as a personal favor? I'll pay you a lot more than you're getting here—and the work isn't as hard."

I was putting on the pressure and I knew it might be a little unfair. If Sam refused, I was in a position to make things uncomfortable for him around the plant. I wouldn't have done this under any circumstances, but Sam had no way of knowing that. Also, in the event of a refusal, he could well be laughed at for being afraid of ghosts when a whole family could take them in stride and when several women from the office had spent the night in the house without witnessing anything unusual. I admit it was unfair, but my conscience was dulled by the necessity of the moment.

Sam agreed to consider it. The next day he informed me that he and Margo had talked it over and that they were willing to work for us.

They turned out to be the best of the help to date. For some reason they were not bothered by anything —or anyone—for quite a while. Dorothy informed Margo that she would take care of the library, herself, and that we had closed off the third floor. We genuinely liked Sam and Margo and they seemed to like us.

There was only one place that Sam refused to go into by himself and that was the furnace room in the basement. I never questioned him about his decision. I had reached the stage where I was willing to let well enough alone. So Sam avoided the basement whenever he could. I remember returning home one day to see Sam and Janet emerging from the basement into the kitchen. Janet was holding firmly onto Sam's hand.

"I went down in the basement with Sam" she confided happily. "We looked at the furnace. I was taking care of him."

I stared quizzically at Sam, but he wasn't even embarrassed. After that, when he had to go to the furnace room, Janet was his companion. Perhaps he felt that her guardian angel would be on the job and her protection would extend to him, also. At any rate "looking after Sam" became little towheaded Janet's self-imposed job. I told myself if this kept Sam happy and on the job, as well as easier in his mind, I couldn't object. A couple of months went by without incident and we were beginning to relax. Dorothy looked more rested and happier.

Margo was one of the most beautiful girls I have ever seen. She was also honest and sweet. However, her beauty was not enough to insulate her against Sam's temper when he was aroused. The day finally came when Sam neglected a certain repair to the furnace (probably because it required his presence down there in the basement for quite some time and Janet was busy elsewhere). The resultant damage cost me quite a bit of money, but Sam claimed complete innocence. He said he had carried out my instructions to the letter but something else went wrong. It was an uneasy Margo who informed me of Sam's negligence.

"I shouldn't tell on Sam," she confessed unhappily. "But he said he'd messed up the repairs you ordered 'cause he didn't want to spend any more time down there. He was afraid. So it wasn't your fault, Mr. Cameron—what went wrong, I mean."

That wasn't Sam's story. I mentioned it to him later on.

That night I heard a slamming noise from the servants' quarters and went up to investigate. Sam was yelling unintelligibly when I opened the door. He had his hands around Margo's throat and was banging her head against the wall.

"I'll kill you, woman! I'll kill you good. You told on me to Mr. Cameron! You're goin' to die, and it won't be a natural death! I'll pound your head to jelly! You won't tell on me no more!"

"Sam!" I shouted. "What's going on?"

He quickly released his hold on Margo's throat and made a visible effort at self-control. "Just an argument, Mr. Cameron," he managed to mumble. "Just a family argument. 'T'aint nothin' serious!"

"Well, we will have no more of this kind of argument. You ought to be ashamed! Margo is no match for an ex-Marine—and a commando, at that!"

I went back downstairs and there was silence from Sam's quarters for the balance of the night. The next morning Margo moved stiffly and had difficulty in turning her head.

"What's the trouble, Margo?" I asked. "Neck bothering you?"

She looked me straight in the eye. "It's of no account, Mr. Cameron. I must have slept in a draft."

I reminded myself that it had been a family argument after all and if this was Margo's attitude, then I had no right to interfere. But, because of this, when just a few nights later, I heard the noise of what seemed like a door slamming again and again, I ran upstairs wondering what Margo had done this time to arouse her husband's anger.

I opened the door and Sam nearly jumped me. He was sitting on the edge of the bed in a crouching position, arms extended in commando fashion, as he waited for me to enter. When he saw who it was, he relaxed, but he still wasn't happy.

"Boss," he said grimly. "That's the fifth time the

door has opened by itself tonight and the first time anyone has been there!"

I grasped the situation at once. It was pure supposition on my part but I couldn't help wondering if our unseen lady had objected to Sam's assault on his wife and was taking this method of chastising him.

"Well, don't worry," I said. "You know how things go on around here once in a while." I looked for Margo then and saw that she was in bed with the covers over her head.

"Yes, I know," Sam replied woodenly. "I've found out. And it ain't just an old wives' tale, either, Mr. Cameron. We just can't take it anymore. I'm sorry, but that's the way it is!"

Sam couldn't be talked out of his decision to leave and Margo, in spite of his temper, adored him. So we lost the only couple who had ever worked out since we moved into the house. They not only left the mansion, but they left the area and returned to Margo's home in Louisiana.

Our first year in the house had ended. Again I was faced with the necessity of getting help for Dorothy. She simply couldn't manage the big place by herself with all the cleaning, washing, ironing, bed-making, cooking, and baby care involved. She was doing physical labor from early morning until late at night and I knew she couldn't keep up the pace indefinitely. I also knew that she would keep on trying. She insisted on an orderly home.

"A disorderly house is an indication of a disorderly mind," she often said.

I was pretty grim about it, however. It was even getting difficult to persuade her to take time out to eat a leisurely meal with the rest of the family. Something had to be done. The solution to my problem came from a totally unexpected source and the solution had been there for weeks. I just hadn't realized it.

6

Enoch

It was during one of my trips down to the old red barn where some of the furniture was stored that I first caught sight of an ancient black man. He didn't appear too friendly and almost dissolved before my eyes in his anxiety to get away. Evidently he wanted no conversation with a stranger. However, as I ran into him from time to time and always spoke pleasantly and acted as if it was the most natural thing in the world for him to be hanging out in the barn, he gained more confidence. One afternoon he actually hesitated when he saw me so I stopped and spoke to him.

"Hello, there!" I hailed.

He hesitated. "Hello, Boss."

"I've seen you a lot down here. You living in the barn?"

He nodded. "That's right, Boss."

"What's your name?" I asked.

"Enoch."

"Now that's a good Bible name," I observed. "I know all about the Bible, you know. My dad is a Baptist preacher and I nearly became one myself. I'm Harold Cameron. I'm glad to meet you, Enoch."

He studied me sideways for a minute and then smiled a pleased sort of smile. He held out his hand and I solemnly shook it.

That was the extent of our first conversation, but I ran into him on the path again. This time I learned that he had been sleeping in the barn, with no other place to go. When I mentioned that it might be pleasant enough in the barn during the summer, but winter might well tell a different story, a shadow fell on his wrinkled old face.

"I been thinking 'bout that," he admitted.

"Well, don't worry. Barns aren't too cold and I'll see that you get plenty of blankets and some provisions, too, if you need them," I promised.

He looked at me in pleased amazement. "You're mighty nice to do that, Boss," he exclaimed.

On my next trip down, I ran into him again and then I felt sure he had been waiting for me.

"Hello there, Enoch!"

"Hello, Boss!"

I feigned fatigue and took out a handkerchief to wipe my forehead. "I've been going pretty hard today, Enoch, and I'd like to rest a bit. Why don't we sit down here and visit for a while?"

We sat on the ground and I noticed that even though he was old and very thin (he could scarcely weigh more than ninety pounds fully clothed), he seemed wiry and tough enough to get through many winters.

"How long have you lived around here, Enoch?"

"All my life. Yes, sir! All my life."

"And how old are you?"

He frowned. "I don't rightly remember how old—but it's a lot more than ninety. Closer to a hundred when I figger things out."

Enoch seemed proud of the fact that he'd probably make it to the century mark. I found myself as excited as he was proud. If he had been in the neighborhood for nearly a hundred years, he was the person to question about the old mansion. I wondered where to start.

"I live in the big house, you know," I remarked casually.

"I know," he replied briefly. There was a closed-in look on his face at the very mention of the place and I had an inner warning to go slow here. I didn't want to rush things. Reluctantly, I changed the subject.

"I haven't forgotten about the blankets," I informed him. "I didn't think you needed them just yet and I wouldn't want rats to get at them if you stored them just any old place."

"It won't be any old place," he assured me. "And there ain't any rats—not with Butch around."

"Is Butch a cat?"

He looked his scorn. "Butch is my dog. He's part mastiff—and he's my best friend."

I imagined that during cold nights he had snuggled up close to his best friend for warmth. I made a mental note to remember Butch when I bought food for Ching and Chang.

"We ain't got rats in the barn, but I got me a mouse," Enoch announced proudly.

"A mouse?" I echoed. "What for?"

"A pet mouse. Not scared a bit. Butch likes him, too."

I chuckled. "You certainly have an interesting family."

"Yep. Keeps a guy from gettin' too lonesome."

One thing about Enoch that had interested me from the start was the fact that he was immaculately clean. He wore faded old denims. They were threadbare in places, but they were clean. His old blue shirt —faded and worn—was also spotless. I wondered how he managed to look so neat and clean under the circumstances in which he was living. It certainly testified to a strict early training. I respected him the more for it.

Cautiously, I brought the subject around to the mansion again. "You ever been in my house, Enoch?"

"Lotsa times. Why?"

"I just wondered. I love the old mansion, myself."

He swung around to stare at me. "You love it?" He sounded so amazed that I found myself on the defensive.

"Sure. There's a lot of atmosphere about an old mansion. Any reason why I shouldn't love it?"

The odd look crossed his face again and he scrambled to his feet. "I gotta go now, Boss. I got things to do." With that he was gone, leaving me mystified and exasperated.

I told Dorothy about our meeting later that evening. "It's got me going," I admitted. "Here's a guy who can give us all the answers—and I have a feeling he isn't about to do it. I think he's scared."

"All you have to do is win his confidence," Dorothy replied. "It may take time—but time is something we have plenty of—at least for the next year."

"It all ties in," I mused. "I feel that something violent and vicious and hidden has to account for these hauntings—for the dark cloud over this place. I've been doing a lot of reading. You know why old castles and old houses are haunted the world over? Because they are old. Because things have happened there.

Evil has often been done with the impetus of raw emotional force."

She blinked a little. "Raw force?"

"Look at it this way," I said. "Creative force just *is*. It could be used the wrong way as well as the right and wouldn't a thought that directed a vicious action leave a sort of vibrational pattern in the ethers—like a sooty thumbprint on a white piece of paper?"

"I guess it could," she conceded. "The older I get, the more I realize how much I don't know."

I grinned. "Then there's hope for you, Honey. It's these people who know it all that are a pain in the neck! But seriously," I went on, "isn't it possible that the directed force—backed with strong emotion—would have to exhaust itself? Even though it might take years of time as we know it before the force is spent?"

"You may be right, Harold. I wouldn't know. But what connection does this have with our mansion?"

"I think there is a connection. Maybe we have some entities here that are trapped in an emotional vortex. Maybe patterns have to be repeated until the force is spent. You told me, yourself, that you felt our unseen visitors might be in trouble. Now I have the feeling that if I could just find out the true history of this place, I'd have the key—be in a better position to handle certain things."

"Well, don't let it become an obsession with you," she advised calmly. "You have other important things to occupy your mind. In the meanwhile, things are going along pretty much all right, aren't they?"

"That they are. But do you realize that we've never had a conversation like this in our entire married life?"

She nodded. "That's true enough."

"And I know something else," I added.

"Now what?"

"I'm hungry!"

She laughed. "Dinner's in the oven. It will be on the table in half an hour," she promised.

It was the day after Sam and Margo left that I had yet another talk with Enoch. This time he had wandered up toward the house and I invited him into the summerhouse for a chat. I was feeling disturbed about the resumption of our servant problem and welcomed an opportunity to talk to Enoch and, maybe, to be more successful in my probing about the past history of the mansion.

"Somethin' botherin' you, Boss?" Enoch asked, his keen old eyes on my face.

"Yes," I replied. "Sam and Margo have left us."

He gave me a shrewd look. "Why?"

I shrugged wearily. "Same old thing, I guess. People are afraid of the house. Nothing has ever happened to any of us in it. We aren't afraid. What's the matter with people, anyway? It seems that they just don't have faith in a God that can protect them and deliver them from evil."

Enoch looked thoughtful. "Maybe. Some things, though, we feel are too much for God to bother himself about down here."

"Well, that's wrong," I said emphatically. "But faith is something each person has to have for himself, I guess. You can't have it for anybody else. That's a big house, Enoch. It's too much house for my wife to have to keep up by herself."

"I know that, Boss. I used to work up there."

I stared at him. "You worked there?" I echoed. "What did you do?"

"I was young then. I was a sort of man-of-all-works,

as they say. I cleaned and swept and dusted and took care of the beds. I cooked a little, too. I'm a good cook."

"You even cooked?" I repeated incredulously.

"Sure 'nuff."

"Tell me about yourself, Enoch." An idea was floating around in my head but I wanted it to settle a little. "You must have had a mighty fine mother—you keep so neat and clean—you're an upstanding person."

He brightened. "Oh, I had a fine mama, all right." He settled down with a reminiscent look on his face. At last Enoch seemed willing to talk about the past.

"My mama loved the Bible. She read me a lot from it," he started after a moment's reflection. "She could read—the folks who owned her taught her that. She went to church regular. She made me learn a lot of the Bible. I know whole pages by heart. I know Genesis, Job, and the Twenty-third Psalm. She was always mighty particular 'bout my raisin'. She wanted me to have faith in God, too, 'cause I'd never know when I was goin' to need Him. You see, she always feared I'd be sold as a slave and would be gone from her forever. It didn't happen that way. God took her himself, instead. Oh, she was a mighty fine mama!"

"Enoch," I asked abruptly. "Don't you ever get lonesome down in the barn by yourself?"

He looked a little injured. "I ain't by myself. I told you 'bout my family—Butch and my mouse. We know each other real well."

"But you need folks, too, Enoch. Everyone does. How about going to work for me?" He looked very startled and I hurried on with my pitch before he could argue against it. "You don't need to do the heavy work at all. What I need is someone in the house in the daytime to help Dorothy and if you could cook some and serve meals—that would be wonderful. I'll pay you well," I went on as he still hesitated. "Then when we move away, you will have some money of your own."

He was thoughtful for a long time and I held my breath. Then he turned to me questioningly. "Did you say daytime, Boss?" he asked point-blank. "I could still sleep in the barn with Butch and my mouse?"

"You can sleep anywhere you want to if you'll help out during the day. You can leave just as soon as dinner is over. We eat as early as we can."

Once again I put a request on a personal basis. "Enoch, please come—as a favor to me. I need you badly." I didn't intend to remind him that he owed me a favor because of the help I was giving him. I didn't have to. As he had said, himself, his mama had brought him up right.

"I'd be right proud to work for you, Boss," he said at last. I heaved an immense sigh of relief.

"I'll get you some clothes," I promised. "A couple of pairs of new blue pants and some white shirts. I'll get them right away."

"New clothes?" He looked down at his worn-out jeans, with a button missing at a strategic place. "Gosh, Boss, I ain't had nothin' new for a long time now."

"Well, that's over," I assured him. Mentally I added socks, shoes, and underwear to the list I was making —and a warm sweater.

"When do you want me?"

"How about six in the morning? I'll let you in the kitchen door. We'll give Dorothy a surprise with some hot coffee when she comes downstairs in the morning."

He grinned. "Okay, Boss."

So we hired Enoch who was as good as his boast when it came to cooking and cleaning. Because he was so slight, he wore one of Dorothy's aprons when he worked in the kitchen. He wasn't about to get any spots on his new clothes. The boys liked Enoch and little Janet tagged after him like a puppy. Sometimes he recited passages from the Bible to her. You could tell that the little girl meant a lot to him. I had been right. Enoch had been lonely and was proud to have "folks" again.

He had been working for us about a month when I began to tire of the routine of getting up early to let him in the kitchen door.

"Enoch," I finally said, "you know it's going to be cold in the tackroom pretty quick now in spite of the blankets and comforters we've given you. You'll have to walk up here a quarter of a mile every morning. Why don't you just sleep upstairs in the servants' quarters where it's warm and cozy?"

He stood motionless at the stove, not bothering to turn around to face me.

"You'd have conveniences that you don't enjoy in the barn," I pointed out.

"I got all the conveniences I need now, Boss," Enoch replied in an expressionless voice.

I had inspected his quarters. It was a typical place to store tack and other small items. It had a wooden floor, old and uneven but swept clean. I strongly suspected that there were rats in the offing just waiting to escape Butch's watchful eye. Enoch had rigged up an overhead shower of sorts and that was adequate for his daily bathing, but that was all. The water would be icy cold, if not frozen in the pipes, in the dead of winter.

"Then you won't sleep up here?" I asked.

He finally turned around. "Up here in the big

house? No, Boss, I won't. I do my work. But I won't sleep here. Not now . . . not ever. I won't stay after dark!"

There was a finality about his words that I had to accept. After all, getting up to let him in was small payment for what he was doing for us. I hadn't given him a key because under my new security arrangements the doors were bolted on the inside at night. Besides, the fewer keys out, the better.

It occurred to me, then, that it wasn't what might get in the house that bothered Enoch. It was what was already there. So I surrendered as gracefully as I could and continued to let him in at six o'clock. He was never late but would be waiting, no matter the time or the weather.

7

The Crypt on the Hill

I didn't expect old Enoch to be any more perfect than the rest of us. It was after his regular salary started that his particular weakness showed up, although it was to be some time before I recognized it. He was rather fond of gin. Not that he was in a constant state of inebriation. Far from it. He was never late to work, but we gave him Saturday afternoons off and he treated himself to a bottle every payday.

At first I wondered where he got the stuff because he didn't seem to wander into town. Then I learned that the family—the "poor" relatives the real estate agent had mentioned—who owned the barn had political connections. A group of prisoners had been released to work, under supervision, on a construction project and they were being housed on the premises in the old barn. The family benefited because they had cheap labor available and made money on housing the prisoners. We still don't know what the prisoners derived from the arrangement.

One of the prisoners, Rollie, was a painter by trade and he was permitted to do some extra work at night for a certain contractor in town. Thus, he had a little extra money which was spent entirely on booze. Rollie and Enoch struck up a friendship of sorts.

I ran into Rollie one day near the barn. He was staggering around, definitely under the influence, and had a handful of salt which he was scattering before him as he went.

"What are you doing?" I asked curiously.

"I salt 'em," he confided with a sly look. "Long as I can salt 'em they can't get at me."

He was only a step removed from delirium tremens but, as it was a Sunday, I supposed the overseer wasn't paying too much attention to his condition. At any rate Rollie had access to liquor—and so had Enoch.

Our first experience with Enoch in his cups had its humorous aspect. One Saturday afternoon I heard his voice down beyond the garden in the direction of the creek. I hadn't even known that he was anywhere around, but he seemed to be entertaining company. His high-pitched, squeaky voice was louder than I had ever heard it.

"Bob," I said to my son. "Enoch's been carrying on for some time. He seems to have company. Let's see what's going on."

We crept silently among the trees, down through the garden to a clearing where Enoch was holding forth. Finally we saw him. He was precariously balanced on an old stump and was expounding the gospel with great vigor. His audience was composed of the trees around the clearing. Undoubtedly, Enoch must have imagined a group of animated listeners for he was holding forth with all the fervor of a traveling evangelist.

"He is chastened also with pain on his bed and the multitude of his bones with strong pain," Enoch thundered. "So that his life abhorreth bread an' his soul dainty meat. His flesh is consumed away that it can't be seen, and his bones that were not seen stick out! Yea, his soul draweth near unto the grave and his life to the destroyer."

Bob nudged me in the ribs, silently convulsed with laughter. "I know old Enoch is thin as a rail," he whispered. "But I didn't know he was in such bad shape."

"Shush!" I whispered back.

Suddenly Enoch whirled and pointed a finger in our direction. "Ain't it so, brothers an' sisters? Ain't it so?" He answered his own question. " 'Course it's so! The Bible tells us—an' the Bible don't lie!"

I was afraid that he'd seen us, but Enoch then pointed his finger toward heaven. "All flesh shall perish together," he thundered. "An' man shall turn again into dust!"

He jumped from the stump, nearly losing his balance, and paced a few wavering steps in each direction before once more taking up his stance.

"There's no darkness, or shadow of death where the workers of iniquity can hide! He knowest their works, an' he overturns 'em in the night so they're destroyed!"

Again he pointed, but this time in another direction. "Ain't it so, brothers? You know it's so—it's writ in the Holy Book!"

"Gosh!" Bob muttered. "No wonder he's afraid to leave the tackroom at night."

"That's good old-fashioned orthodox doctrine," I

hissed back. "Let's get out of here before he sees us!"

We quietly withdrew and in a few minutes were on our way back to the house.

"Imagine that little guy!" Bob marveled. "What was he quoting?"

"The Book of Job," I replied. "He told me he knew it all and now I believe him. He's been holding forth down there for an hour at least. Quite a feat for someone who can't read or write. There's no doubt that in his soul Enoch longs to be a preacher of the Word."

"Just another frustrated preacher," Bob grinned. "Glad it didn't take you that way."

I only grunted.

We were to have further evidence of Enoch when inebriated, but even then he was a harmless, lovable little gnome of a man. He merely became more loquacious—more voluble—but there was no real belligerence or malice in his make-up.

I seized upon that first opportunity, however, to interrogate Enoch when his defenses were down. Naturally, I hoped he could explain the strange happenings in our old mansion, so I waved Bob on home and waited for Enoch to pass the summerhouse. Finally he came—weaving his way through the trees and clambering over the wall toward where I was sitting.

"How are you, Enoch?" I called. "Taking a little walk on your day off?" I gave no indication that I had heard his sermon.

He looked up, startled. Then he furtively patted the bottle in his hip pocket. "Yes, sir, I was just lookin' over the place—just lookin' aroun'. The garden is doin' right pretty, seems like. I was goin' to get me a mushmelon but they ain't ripe."

"How about sitting down here in the summerhouse, Enoch? You and I seldom have the chance to talk anymore—I've been so busy—you too."

Enoch seated himself carefully on the bench while I tried to find the best way to start the conversation. He had carefully skirted any mention of the phantoms in the big house. I knew that he was our best source of information concerning the history of the place, but he had been as uncommunicative as a sphinx on the subject. Now this seemed like a golden opportunity and I wasn't above taking advantage of it.

"Was your mother here when the place was built, Enoch?" I felt this might be a safe approach.

"No, that was before her time. But she tole me 'bout my granny. She was housemaid for the Murchinsons that built the first house. Good thing she slept in the quarters outside 'stead of in the house or she would have got burned up, too."

"How was that, Enoch? What happened?"

"You know they ain't never been nothin' but bad luck and sorrow in this house," he mourned. "The back part is on the foundation of that first one. It was built only two, three years when it caught fire in the middle of the night. Seven—I think it was—seven of the family burnt up. They're all buried up there on the hill where you see the big tree."

I told myself that his mind was really wandering now—probably the result of too much gin. "Enoch, I've hunted all over that hill shooting woodchuck and I've never come across a graveyard. Are you sure?"

"They's up there all right. The Murchinsons had an underground burial up there. You know that big slab of rock that is just beyond the wooden gate?" He pointed a shaky finger in the direction of the hill. "Right under that rock is where they is. You know it leans over so crazy?"

By way of illustration, Enoch leaned to his left and nearly fell off the bench. I steadied him quickly and he went on. "Well, it used to be straight up and there's a hole that goes down into the burial. I ain't never gone in it, but it's there, all right. I heard tell it was all bricked over with them coffins on shelves. That's where the Murchinsons was buried—and seven of 'em put there all at once when the fire happened."

I looked across the alfalfa fields toward the top of the hill. Even at that distance I could see the wooden gate I had climbed over many times. The gnarled old oak tree stood outlined against the sky. The ground sloped away gently on all sides, making a bald knob with the great oak in its center. The leaning rock was also visible. From where I sat it looked like any peaceful country scene.

"Will you go up and show me, Enoch? I'd like to explore that underground burial place."

Enoch fairly jumped out of his skin. "No, sir, I won't!" he cried in anguish. I had the feeling that he was sobering up quickly. "I don't want to go! I never did go down in there—I just heard 'bout it. That old stone slab fell down when I was just a young fella. By then the big house had been built like it is now."

Suddenly Enoch was anxious to talk. Evidently he wanted to get my mind off a place he had no intention of taking me to. "I 'member when the old doctor put in them stain glass windows in the liberry."

"But what's that got to do with the burial place, Enoch?" Then I did a double take. This was the first time I'd heard of a doctor in the mansion.

" 'Twas 'bout that time the slab fell, I reckon. No-

body cared. The Murchinsons was all gone. Ain't nobody been down in there since then. You'd have to dig
under the rock to find the openin' now."

He searched my face and then sighed resignedly.
"Maybe you'd want to go. You ain't scared in the big
house—maybe you ain't scared of that, neither."

"What's there to be scared of in the big house,
Enoch?"

He gulped suddenly. "I gotta be goin'. I gotta go
feed Butch," he mumbled desperately. "He's hungry
by now, I bet." And Enoch ambled off, looking as if
he'd said too much and was already regretting it.

I was busy that following week, but I kept thinking
about Enoch's account of the crypt. Early the next
Saturday morning I cornered Hal who seemed at
loose ends with Bob gone for the weekend.

"What about investigating Enoch's story?" I asked
him. "Want to take a look for that old burial place?"

"Why not?" he agreed.

It was the sort of thing that I knew would interest
Hal. He wasn't nervous in the least. It interested me,
too, but I had another motive. I wanted to test
Enoch's memory of past events. And, to be truthful,
this was the sort of investigation that intrigued me.
It seemed to satisfy that part of me which longed to
identify with historic moments and places in history.

There was a half-mile of alfalfa field and then a
stretch of grass between us and the old wooden
gate. As we hiked, Hal asked, "Do you really think
there are any graves? Do you suppose old Enoch
knows what he's talking about, or is he just trying
to make himself important?"

"I'd say he knows. He's not like a lot of old people

—he doesn't talk about the past very much. The only reason he told me about the crypt was because he was relaxed and talkative after his gin."

Hal laughed. "Bob told me about the sermon. He couldn't get over it. Said Enoch was the reincarnation of Jonathan Edwards."

"That's right. He hadn't gotten around to sinners frying in hell yet. But to get back to this crypt, I had the feeling that Enoch said more than he meant to— and regretted it almost immediately. His tongue was loosened just enough to let a trickle through a dike he wanted to keep closed. Either our Enoch is afraid to talk, or he's keeping secrets for someone's benefit. I think he's afraid, myself. Yes, I do expect to find evidence that he's telling the truth."

We climbed over the gate with its weathered planks and walked toward the slab of rock that Enoch had pointed out. It was five feet long, slanted forward at about a forty-five degree angle with one end buried in the ground. We knelt down and felt around the end of the base. Grass had grown over it; winds had blown in weeds and debris.

Suddenly Hal whistled. "Dad, I think there's an indentation here. Let's pull these weeds away and see!"

We worked diligently for about ten minutes and then we could see where the ground had unmistakably sunk in one place.

"What now?" Hal asked.

"Back to the house," I told him. "We'll get a couple of spades and a ladder. If it's as Enoch described, we'll need to climb down into the place but I think you're right. This must be the old entrance. No one just walking by would ever find it!"

As we approached the house, we saw Enoch peering out of an upstairs window and as soon as we entered the kitchen, he came haltingly down the stairs.

"I seen you go up the hill," he said, troubled. "You ain't goin' back there again, are you?"

"Yes, we are, Enoch. We're going to take a spade and a ladder and have a look. Do you think we can get down there?"

He grasped the banister for support and stood still for a moment as if searching for words. Then they came in a rush but his voice was shakier than usual.

"Don't go in there, Boss! Don't bother them people. They been gone more'n a hundred years. Nobody done disturbed them in all this time! Nobody but me knew they was there." He broke into a wail. "Now I done it! O, Lawdy, I done it! Me an' my big mouth!"

"But Enoch," I protested.

"Please don't pester them people. Let 'em be!"

At last I understood why Enoch was so reticent about talking of the phantoms in the old house. He was terrified of them.

"Why are you so afraid, Enoch? Do you think these people come down to the house at night? Are they the restless spirits that trouble this place? Is this the reason you won't sleep in the house in a good bed? You can trust me. I really want to know."

Enoch turned to go up the stairs. Then he hesitated and turned back. "No, Boss, they ain't the ones. But they might be should you stir 'em up! 'Nuff goes on already without that. But I don't know nuthin' 'bout it. I don't know nuthin' at all!"

He went on up the stairs, mumbling to himself.

As Hal and I returned up the slope with ladder, spades, and flashlights, we knew that Enoch was watching from an upstairs window. I seemed to feel his eyes boring into my back as we continued up the hill. I began to be a little uneasy—not because I shared Enoch's fear of the burial place—but for fear he'd get so upset that he'd quit his job. That would be too big a price to pay for curiosity. Hal finally broke the silence between us.

"Dad, do you suppose this could be where the night visitor comes from? The man who walks right by the coach house sometimes? He could come from the hill."

"I don't know," I admitted. "I tell myself that I don't believe in ghosts, but crazy things keep happening whether I believe in them or not. However, Enoch said they didn't come from the hill and he ought to know. I think he knows who the two we hear really are, too."

Hal shook his head moodily. "Well, it's darned peculiar, anyway," he observed. "I'd like to get at the truth as much as you would. We don't have courses on this sort of thing in college."

"It might be good if you did," I replied. "Then maybe the people these things happen to wouldn't be made to feel like social outcasts."

Soon we were back at the base of the leaning stone and we went to work. We carefully removed the sod as I intended to leave the place as much like we found it as we could. We dug through more debris and exposed what had been definitely an opening. The steps leading downward had crumbled and given away. Although it was pitch dark beneath us, I played the beam of my flashlight downward. There was quite obviously a large room below that extended to our right from the foot of the marker stone. Enoch had been right! It was a brick-walled enclosure with a gothic arch overhead and had been sturdily constructed.

We enlarged the opening and inserted the ladder.

I admitted to a few goose pimples, but I told myself that an underground graveyard shouldn't be spookier than the usual church cemetery or even the above-ground crypts in New Orleans. I looked at Hal for a moment and took a deep breath.

"Well, here goes!" I said in what I hoped was a matter of fact tone.

"Watch your step!" Hal warned needlessly. I went down first and he followed.

Gingerly we lowered ourselves into the crypt which turned out to be a room about twenty feet long and only ten feet high. When I finally stood on the floor of the eerie place and turned my flashlight upward in order to examine the top, it looked frighteningly high and far away. The air in the crypt was stale and fetid. Iron pipes remained, rusted but still intact, which formed the base for wooden platforms on which caskets had rested. But down the length of both sides the wooden supports had rotted and fallen and the caskets had disintegrated. On the floor could be seen piles of bones and scattered remnants of wood as well as fragments of cloth and silver or pewter handles that had once been attached to the sides of the caskets. Here and there among the bones, a skull glistened.

At the moment I could think of a very valid reason for cremation—it's clean and quick.

"Who would believe this?" I asked. My voice seemed to disturb a stillness that had prevailed for many years. I was glad that Enoch had declined to accompany us. I leaned forward and secured a souvenir. This was a silver handle from a casket. I wanted to prove to myself later on that we really had been in this unbelievable place, this contrast to the peaceful rolling hill above us. Hal did the same thing and was curiously examining his find by the light of his own flash.

I raised my head and, as I did so, my light reflected on the rounded arch above me. It was moving with a circular motion. I waited a few seconds, conscious of a feeling of dizziness and nausea. Then I gasped a warning to Hal. "Let's get out of here!"

We scrambled up the ladder—at least we tried to, but our knees were weak and we were gasping for air. After I had pulled Hal up the remaining steps, we collapsed on the grass and lay there for several moments, realizing what a narrow escape it had been.

"Thank you, God!" I said fervently.

"What happened down there?" Hal's face was white. "I sort of jumped when you told me to, but I barely got up that ladder."

"No oxygen," I answered, still taking deep breaths of precious air. "We used up what little came through the opening. It wasn't enough. When that ceiling started moving around, it was evidence of my dizzy reaction in that stale atmosphere. Thank God I was conscious enough to realize the danger!"

"And thank you, too, Dad," Hal said quietly.

I felt in my pocket where I had thrust the casket handle. "Where's your souvenir?" I asked him.

"I dropped it," he replied grimly. "And I'm not going back for it, either!"

When we felt better, we pulled up the ladder. Then we covered up the entrance, replaced the turf and made our way back home. Both of us were still considerably shaken.

"You know, Dad," Hal said soberly. "We could both have died down there and no one would have known where to look for us. I didn't tell Mom where we were going."

"Neither did I," I admitted. "I don't think she would have approved any more than Enoch did. But he would have known where to look for us."

"That's small comfort," replied Hal shortly.

I knew what he meant. Enoch would have known, but if we had failed to return would he have told of our planned expedition—or would he have been too scared, believing that those spirits we had disturbed had taken care of us in their own fashion? He might also have believed that if they were riled up to that extent, even talking about them would bring swift retribution on his head. In that case, Enoch might have remained silent and simply left the house. After all, he had been the one responsible for our going there in the first place. He and his big mouth.

I only knew that we had a narrow brush with death that bright Saturday morning and were fortunate to be alive. I thought about the blessed privilege of being able to breathe as we neared the mansion. At the moment, all secrets of the past and my own curiosity regarding them were forgotten.

8

Bits and Pieces

After our visit to the crypt on the hill, Enoch was apprehensive for days. He would watch us covertly to see if we continued in good health or acted strangely in any way. He was unusually alert for noises around the house and seemed more nervous than usual. As time passed, however, with no incidents as an aftermath of what Enoch had termed our "discommoding of them people," he grew more friendly and was more at ease. He was obviously relieved that our visit hadn't "stirred them up," as he had feared. I was also conscious of a sort of grudging respect on his part, for it seemed that I had done something that he could admire, if not emulate.

Later on, I pondered over Enoch's words that had been spoken in fear and apprehension. He had been emphatic in his statement that our phantoms in the mansion itself were not the same as those on the hill. He had only feared more ghostly manifestations in a house that had enough things going on in it already.

If it hadn't been for this conviction of Enoch's, I would have been convinced that our visitors had come from the old crypt. Certainly the tragedy connected with the first building could be the basis for such events. But Enoch had said they weren't the same —leading to the logical conclusion that he knew who our mansion visitors were. Our problem was to gain his confidence. I still felt he was the only living person I might contact who could enlighten us on our mystery. He had worked in the house since he was "knee high," as he said, and what he hadn't witnessed himself, he would have learned from family discussion. Thus, the most important thing to do now was to cultivate Enoch's friendship. Our motives weren't entirely ulterior, either, because we all liked Enoch for himself. He, in turn, remained quietly unobtrusive during the day, going efficiently about his work, and returning to the tackroom each night—as soon as it grew dark.

It was Enoch who identified Old Mattie for us. This ancient crone who was apparently demented sometimes appeared, walking about the place dressed in a strange outfit. It was dirty, loose, flowing. She had numerous pockets pinned up in the folds of this garment in which she hid all sorts of things—pieces of string, bottle tops, bits of metal or cloth that she spied lying about. She only came near the house once, but that once was enough. At that time she stood on the gravel path beneath the front window, shaking her fist and screaming epithets.

"Get out of my house!" she yelled. "You've no business here! It's mine! Get out—or you'll be sorry!" Then she broke into obscenities that made Dorothy back hastily away from the window and brought Enoch to her side in a protective manner.

"Who's that old witch?" I demanded angrily.

"That's just Ole Mattie. She ain't right in the head," Enoch replied.

"What's she doing around here? What does she mean this is her house?"

I had already determined that she was definitely in the flesh—and dirty flesh at that. It was a new experience for us. Here we were faced with an apparition—but this was one we could actually see!

"She lived here a long time ago," Enoch replied. "But she don't rightly own nuthin'. Her people—they just feed her and that's all."

"Does she ever come down to the barn, Enoch?"

He gave a small grin. "Once in a while she come down at night. Couple of times she crawled into bed with Butch an' me."

I blinked. "What did you do then?" I asked curiously.

"Me? I just tumbled out the other side, that's what I did," he answered emphatically. "I got Butch trained now so he don't let her in no more."

So much for Enoch's virtue, I thought. But as we couldn't depend on Butch being in two places at once and we weren't sure we could let the chows stay out unsupervised at night, I phoned the agent and complained of the visitation.

"You tell the owners to take care of this," I ordered shortly. "It's one thing we don't have to tolerate—and we don't intend to!"

After that she never came up to the house, but we did glimpse her once in a while in the woods and down near the barn, picking up her treasures and

stowing them away. Old Mattie lent yet another touch
of local color to the mansion, but it was color we
could do without.

Proof of Enoch's evasiveness and caution was the
fact that we had lived in the big house for months
before we even knew of his existence. Up to that
time he had been an elusive shadow when spotted at
all—a shadow with no personality or features. I was
to learn more about Enoch as I gradually won his
confidence and continued to ignore his "happy hours"
after payday. One Saturday he approached me in his
shy and diffident manner.

"Boss," he asked in a low voice, looking around to
see if we were alone. "Could you please take me in
your car 'bout three miles down the road?"

"Of course, Enoch," I replied. "Just where do you
want to go?"

He grinned in a conspiratorial manner, then answered, half-proudly, "I want to see my girl friend."

It took me at least thirty seconds to recover. A dog
and a mouse I could accept as companions for a man
approaching the century mark. A woman shocked me.

"Why, sure, Enoch," I replied weakly when I got my
breath back. "You bet I'll take you. And if you'll tell
me when you want to come back, I'll pick you up,
too."

Enoch disappeared and came back with his straw
hat on. He was wearing his white shirt and one of his
new pairs of blue pants. He climbed into the car and
we were off.

"What's her name?" I asked him in a kidding manner. "Delilah?"

I should have known better than to pull that line
with Enoch who knew all about Delilah, and Jezebel,
too. "Nuthin' like that, Boss," he replied with dignity.

"Her name is Willie Mae and she's a right smart gal—a fine figger of a woman."

"Bigger than you are, Enoch?"

"Shucks, yes! Willie Mae 'bout two hundred fifty pounds, Boss. We're real good friends. We got insurance on each other."

"You mean if anything happens to you, she gets the cash and if anything happens to her, you get it?"

"Yep. Every dime," he agreed, as if it were something to be proud of.

I thought about Enoch's financial condition when I offered him the job. "But when you aren't working—who pays the premiums?" I demanded.

"Oh, she pays 'em. She's a real good friend."

"Mind telling me how old she is, Enoch?" I thought if she was near his own age and this relationship had gone on for some years that it might not be such a bad arrangement at that. At least funeral expenses would be taken care of.

"She's young—real young—she ain't fifty yet."

I had a little trouble keeping the car on the road and took my foot off the gas pedal in surprise. This was something that would take a little thinking about but I changed the subject because I didn't want Enoch to think I was prying into his personal affairs.

"Enoch, the other day you mentioned a doctor who put in the stained glass windows in the library. He must have been quite a fellow."

"Yessir. He was a nice man, all right. But the Missus really had it done. She was sure one for nice things. I was workin' in the house then like I do now and everything had to be just so. In them days the two big lights in the liberry had to be dusted every week an' kept sparkly. We had to shine them floors 'til you could see your face in 'em. She sure did want that liberry just so and she had it fixed up real pretty."

I felt a surge of excitement. "So the Doctor did just what she wanted—is that it?"

"Yessir. 'Bout everybody done what she said. She was sure one for gettin' her own way."

Enoch paused for a moment as if searching his memory. At last he was talkative and relaxed. I silently blessed Willie Mae and his impending visit with her for this unexpected change of attitude. He went on easily.

" 'Twas her what had the summerhouse built. She had more flowers 'round than anyone. Most all was roses. She had roses climbin' all over that summerhouse."

"She must have been an unusual woman. How long ago was that, Enoch?"

He squinted. "Long time back. Hard to tell. I was just young then. I slept in the old quarters. They're all gone now—all torn down and gone long ago. But I worked in the house. I was always helpin' the cook and sweepin' floors and makin' beds. I remember that all right. We learned to work real young then, seems like." He gave a sigh.

"Must have been around eighty-six or eighty-seven years ago, then?"

"Sumthin' like that," he agreed. Then he leaned forward and touched my arm, indicating a driveway. I was sorry we had arrived at our destination so soon for I felt the conversation might prove to be fruitful. But now I was sure of the identity of the unseen lady in our house. She was still particular about her library and, judging from Ernestine's experience, she was still headstrong about getting her own way.

We drove into the yard of a pretentious home—

one that was characteristic of the vicinity. Hat in hand, Enoch knocked at the back door. I had a glimpse of a large black woman as the door opened. She and Enoch exchanged a few words and then he came back to the car.

"I'll stay here a while," he told me. "There's nobody home right now and I want to visit with Willie Mae. You don't need to wait."

"I'll tell you what," I said. "I have business at the office. I'll drive in and take care of it now. Then I'll pick you up on my way back. It will be at least two hours."

Enoch was grateful. "I'll be waitin' out in front," he promised. "If I ain't there, I'll be startin' to walk home and be down the road a piece."

He went back into the house and I drove off, chuckling to myself. I wondered what the family would say to this latest bit of news about Enoch. None of us had ever seen Enoch with Willie Mae and I didn't expect we ever would, but that would be a sight to behold! Little Enoch, only five foot two when he stood on tiptoe, and this young giantess. If this relationship was on the up-and-up, the romantic involvement couldn't happen to a more deserving fellow. They must have something in common, I told myself. I hoped it wasn't just the insurance policies because it was obvious that Willie Mae would get the better of that deal. I would have given a lot to know whose idea the policies were and whether the original suggestion had come from Enoch or his Willie Mae—or even from an ambitious insurance agent.

True to his promise, I found Enoch a couple of hours later just around the bend in the road and trudging toward home. He climbed gratefully into the car and seemed in good humor. I got a strong whiff of gin on his breath and thought that it must have been payday for Willie Mae, too. Either that or she'd helped herself from someone's liquor cabinet.

I picked up our conversation where I had dropped it a couple of hours ago.

"Enoch, did you ever hear of a tunnel of any kind —a sort of shortcut—that led up to the mansion?"

He thought a moment. "No—never did," he replied at last.

"I was thinking about the springhouse," I said.

Behind the house there was a drop of some hundred feet—too steep to be negotiated by foot. However, a well-defined path wound down over to the side of this sharp incline and ended up at the springhouse which was used in the old days to keep dairy products cold and also for storage of perishables. Beyond the springhouse one could follow the path to the barn where Enoch slept. There might have been an original tunnel leading to the mansion from the springhouse—and I said as much to Enoch.

"Don't know nuthin' 'bout it," he confessed and I felt he was telling the truth. "Could be, I 'spose, but I don't know. But they kept runaway slaves at the house. It was a sort of station."

Again I felt a stir of excitement. "Runaway slaves!" I echoed. "Those must have been amazing days, Enoch."

"Mebbe so, but I was too young to know much. Folks didn't talk—they didn't dare. Sometimes I knew someone was bein' kept some place in the big house and the next day he'd be gone. Sometimes there be more'n one. An' sometimes they was sick or hurt and I'd have to clean up blood in the kitchen. I was told not to ask questions 'cause it was safer I didn't know nuthin'. So I didn't ask." He was silent for a moment and then gave me a sideways glance. "My mama said that most people's troubles was 'cause they didn't know 'nuff to keep their mouth shut."

So Enoch had been taught discretion at an early age. As far as I could see, he was still taking his mama's advice.

"But you know, Enoch, there could well be a secret room in the old house. We've looked all over, but we haven't found it."

"Why you want to find it, Boss? You need another room?" Enoch sounded incredulous and I didn't blame him.

"No, of course not. But it might be the answer to some of the things that go on. Maybe someone could come into the house by a secret way and—well—do things."

Enoch lost his geniality. "Them as comes into the big house don't need no secret way," he said grimly.

His reminiscing was definitely over for the day, but I was grateful for the bits and pieces he had furnished. I knew there was much more to learn and it was going to take time and patience to get it out of Enoch but at least some of his reticence had given away under my persistent and sometimes offhand questioning. In spite of Dorothy's advice not to get too involved, I felt that I was becoming obsessed with the necessity for finding out what had happened in that mansion. It was as if the place was a great gray spider in the midst of a torn web and I was trying to repair the old web.

I reported the events of the afternoon to Dorothy after we had gone to bed. She laughed indulgently over my account of Enoch's courtship.

"Did you see the woman?" she asked.

"Just a glimpse, but I'd know her again, I'm sure."

"Who thought up the insurance deal?"

"I don't know yet. I'm not too happy about it, either. I hope someone is looking out for Enoch's interests."

"Well," she remarked. "I suppose it's really none of our business. He seems to be happy with the arrangement and that's what counts. Did you find out anything else?"

"I found out that our house was once a station for runaway slaves," I announced triumphantly. "Enoch remembers something of that but was cautioned to keep quiet—to keep out of trouble. Then there was a doctor and his wife. They lived here when Enoch worked in the house when he was very young. Now get this! The wife was a headstrong lady who always got her own way. She was inordinately proud of the library and kept the servants busy shining chandeliers, polishing floors and furniture. She had her husband install the stained glass windows. She also had him build the summerhouse and she was very fond of flowers—roses were her favorites. She had more flowers than anyone else around."

I could sense Dorothy's concentration. She finally murmured, "This woman had determination and drive —and was overly fond of her library. She loved flowers and would naturally feel that they were a gracious gift. Well, I suppose that's it."

"Has to be!" I stated positively. "And it was over eighty-five years ago, according to Enoch."

"But Harold!" Dorothy cried in a distressed voice. "That isn't enough! Pride in a home and love for flowers—even a headstrong nature—our world is full of these human attributes. That isn't enough to keep an individual chained to a spot all of these years!"

"No," I agreed gently. "I'm afraid it isn't. And it isn't enough to scare the wits out of Enoch, either."

"Perhaps we're better off not knowing what really happened. Maybe we're prying—interfering—sort of."

"They interfered with us first," I reminded her a little tartly.

"They did at that," she admitted. "Well, I do know one thing! We don't lead a dull life!"

"Sorry?" I asked.

"Never!" she replied stoutly.

I gave her hand a little squeeze and went on thoughtfully. "Then let's look at the facts we do have. We are living in a house that went through the tragedy of a fire with seven unexpected and untimely deaths; a house that was a station for runaway slaves and held all the misery of those days, including fear and violence and panic; then a doctor on the premises who was under the thumb of an impetuous, headstrong wife who was mistress of this place and had an obsession about her library. Some sort of emotional background is beginning to emerge."

"But," she insisted, "it isn't enough. What Enoch has kept quiet about must be the real crux of the hauntings." She hesitated and then went on slowly. "Something must have created what you called the power vortex—the whirlwind of negative and terrible emotions that act now as a magnet for unseen entities. Maybe there are more of them than we realize, too!"

"I thought of that," I admitted. "But then I didn't *want* to think of it. But I'll bet you're thinking right now of Hal's experience the other night."

"Yes, I am. I'm trying to reconcile the fact that sometimes doors are opened and knobs turn while, at other times, whoever wants to, simply comes in."

Hal's experience had puzzled me, too. There had been a college dance and when he arrived home, he didn't feel particularly sleepy. He went into the living room and listened to some records for a while. Then he decided that he was hungry because refreshments had been on the light side. He went to the kitchen and was fixing himself a sandwich when he heard a slight noise, like a mouse nibbling. He looked over at the basement door and saw the knob turn back and forth as it had done the night my sister had been with us. He put the sandwich down and noiselessly removed his shoes. Then he sped upstairs and shook me awake as the boys had so often done before.

"Dad! Wake up! We've got 'em this time with all those lights in the basement. They can't get away!"

I automatically reached for my slippers. "Got who?" I questioned sleepily.

"Someone in the basement. I heard him. He's trying to get into the kitchen through the door. I saw the knob turning. Hurry!"

I armed myself with a gun. Once in the kitchen, I switched on the basement lights and flung the door open at the same time. As I went down the stairs, Hal stood behind me, blocking the way upstairs but ready to spring to my aid if I needed him. I finally went back to where he was standing, looking dejectedly at me.

"There isn't a soul down here," I told him flatly. "There isn't even a mouse! It's just like that other time, but much easier to see with the bright lights."

"But Dad!" he cried. "This time I heard the noise and I saw that knob turn back and forth for a full half-minute! It couldn't be a ghost. They don't need to open doors. They can go right through."

Together we made another search and then gave up. Back in the kitchen with the door locked once again, Hal finished his sandwich, munching thoughtfully, while I made a cup of coffee. I felt that sleep was forgotten for the night, anyway.

This was one of those contradictions that Dorothy spoke of. Something was always unbalancing my thinking and I couldn't find a parallel in any of the accounts of hauntings that I had read.

"Well," I told Dorothy now, "maybe some entities have more energy than others—more abilities—just as humans have."

"We might as well get some sleep," she sighed.

"Maybe we get instruction in the sleeping state," I ventured. "We know that certain problems are seen in a different light when we wake up."

"I could stand a little instruction on some of the things that go on around here," she admitted. "But my mind has already been stretched in directions I didn't think even existed. I'm not sure that I'm grateful for the exercise, either."

I chuckled. "Unaccustomed exercise has a way of making muscles sore at first. Let's give it time. Who knows—we may develop into mental giants yet?"

As usual she had the last word. "I've never really wanted to meet a giant. I still think they belong in fairy tales."

9

The Secret Room

My brother, Colonel Arthur Cameron, United States Air Force, with an office in the Pentagon, approved of my efforts to find *rational* explanations. At first, he hooted at my suggestion that we might have some invisible entities around. That didn't bother me at all. I would have hooted at it a year earlier, myself.

"Nothing to that, Harold, nothing at all," Arthur assured me breezily. "But I admit you have an interesting problem. I'll be down this weekend to work on it. Mind if I bring Rita?"

"Not at all," I answered.

"The Air Force is landing," I told Dorothy when I turned from the phone. "We can now relax. Everything will be under control in this house."

She laughed. "I take it you were talking to Arthur on the phone?"

"Yes, and he's also bringing Rita. Okay?"

She nodded. "It has to be. I don't know her very

well, but I think she does him more good than he realizes."

Rita was a tall beautiful blonde. She was helping Arthur through a trying time—the trauma of his divorce from my sister-in-law Ernestine, the one who had suffered such a shock in our library. They were later to be married, and Arthur wanted to be sure that we would welcome the girl who was to take Ernestine's place.

Arthur's slightest request carried with it a totalitarian overtone that I associated with many officers in our armed forces. He had the same attitude toward our unseen entities who did not advance, halt, or come to attention on command that he would have exhibited toward refractory cadets.

I am the first to admit that I have many human failings. Where my brother was concerned, I privately hoped that something would happen to shake him out of his complacency. I didn't have long to wait.

The first night that Arthur and Rita were with us was a bright moonlit night, reminiscent of the night that Joe and Carrol had camped in the yard earlier that year.

They were sitting upstairs in one of the big windows that had been opened to the night air. Suddenly their low-voiced conversation was interrupted by the sound of footsteps crunching down on the gravel. Arthur leaned over to see who was coming up to the house so late at night. No form was visible in the bright moonlight. The footsteps, however, came to the front entrance of the house which was just beneath them. They mounted the steps of the porch and ceased abruptly. Mystified, the couple waited for the sound of the front knocker. Nothing happened.

"Who's down there?" The Colonel barked in the voice that had quailed so many cadets. "Speak up!"

There was complete silence. Half-angry and half-puzzled, Arthur went downstairs to look around. Rita followed to the head of the stairs as he switched on the porchlight. There was no one on the front porch and he had to first unlock the door before he opened it. He relocked the door. Then scratching his short-cropped head, he came up to the master bedroom. I was reading in bed while Dorothy was relaxing in a warm tub just a few steps across the hall. This was the one luxury she permitted herself after a busy day.

"Damned if I know what to think," Arthur admitted. "I heard those footsteps plainly and so did Rita, but we didn't see a soul and the moonlight is so bright outside I bet I could read a newspaper out there."

"That's right," Rita agreed. "I heard someone, too. But he stopped at the porch and never did ring the bell. I didn't hear him go away, either."

I put down my book. "I haven't told you a fraction of the things that have gone on around this place," I replied. "You didn't sound too receptive on the phone. But if you think you can find any explanation for them, just go right ahead."

"Someone gets in this house," Arthur stated positively.

"Didn't you check the doors and windows?" I asked. "I always do before I go to bed. Everything was locked up tonight."

"There must be a secret entrance," he mused. "There has to be some place where they can hide. These walls are deep enough to contain a secret passageway."

I grinned even though I was slightly irritated. He had announced his conclusion as if none of us had ever thought of such a thing. "We've taken that into consideration and we've investigated those walls. So far we've come up with nothing to indicate a secret passage. But aren't you getting a little far afield? What started your investigation was the footsteps outside the house and no one to make them. So what if the person was coming through an underground tunnel and through the walls? How could his steps have sounded above him on the gravel? Unless, of course, we have a prehistoric fly walking on the ceiling of a passageway down there."

He ignored my levity. I knew he would. "I don't know yet," he snapped, "but I'm going to find out!" As I remained silent, he looked at me accusingly. "You sound as if you really believe this ghost junk!"

"Listen, my esteemed brother! I'll be glad if you can present me with a logical alternative. More glad than you realize! I've spent months trying to figure things out although I haven't had time to devote to it exclusively. After all, I've got to make a living. But I'm happy to have you poking around at any time. In the meantime, Arthur, I've got a question or two that I've been wanting to ask you in your own field."

"Go ahead!" He was always agreeable when asked for his opinion or his advice.

I thought for a moment, recalling the incident I wanted to discuss. A few days before, I had purchased a plane ticket for Washington, D.C., and was taking an early morning flight from Philadelphia on urgent business. When the time for our departure arrived, we were not permitted to board the plane. A couple of hours passed and we became irate over the unexplained delay. The majority of the passengers were businessmen with important appointments. Some were in the diplomatic service and there was a sprinkling of attorneys. Government appointments were hard to come by in those busy days and simply were not broken.

As a result of our persistent questioning, it was

finally disclosed that there was some unusual activity in the skies above the capital. Unidentified objects had been picked up on the radar screen and no plane could take off or land at the Washington airport until an all-clear signal was given. As yet, we still waited.

Finally, at seven o'clock that night our plane did leave—but not for Washington. We landed at Baltimore and from there went by bus into the city of Washington. We received no further explanation or clarification whatever. A couple of lawsuits were instigated because of that wasted day.

When I told Arthur what had happened, he was obviously uneasy.

"That does occur," he admitted. "More often than the public knows."

"But what are the unidentified flying objects?" I persisted. "Planes from some other country snooping around?"

"No!" he exploded. "We could handle that! These can't be aircraft as we know them—not the way they move around. We haven't anything on our drawing boards that can touch them—even in potential. We don't know what they are or where they come from!"

I was growing more interested. "Another area of phenomena that can't be tested?" I asked.

He was definitely annoyed. "How can you test anything you can't catch up with?" he asked sourly.

I grinned. "My point exactly," I told him. "It just happens that this is in your area of activity. Our mystery is in mine."

"But I can catch up with yours," he argued. "It happens in a definite place."

"Well and good," I said cheerfully. "When you catch up with the guy who walks the gravel paths from the old coach house and with the woman who comes from the library and sometimes carries flowers around in the upstairs hall, hang onto both of them. I deserve first look!"

He finally gave a sheepish grin. "You win!" he admitted. "But I'm still going to look for secret passages and rooms. This idea of ghosts has to be a lot of nonsense."

"Well, this is an historic old place and you may be right. It was once a station for runaway slaves. They had to hide somewhere in the house where they would be undetected in the event of an investigation."

"I'll get at it the first thing in the morning," he promised. "Do you have a steel measuring tape—a long one?"

"Enoch can probably find you one."

"Shall I ask him now?"

"Enoch," I informed him, "does not sleep in the big house. He prefers the barn."

Rita had remained completely silent during our exchange, her blue eyes wide and troubled. Now she only said a sober "Goodnight, Harold." They left the room together and I turned back to my book.

What Arthur didn't realize, however, and what I hadn't felt like confiding, was the fact that my interest now wasn't in physical dimensions but in learning about past events that might serve as a blueprint for the psychic atmosphere that made such phenomena possible. It was like looking at a photograph of a family group. Most people would be busy identifying those they knew in the picture. I was searching the background for an unfamiliar or fuzzy face peering around a tree or looking down from an obscure window.

The next morning Arthur started over what was by now a familiar route to the rest of us. Rita trailed along. He tapped walls and measured dimensions of rooms. He looked up sooty fireplaces. He searched for movable panels. He went outside and measured every wall and alcove of the house, making neat rows of figures in a little book over which he pored industriously. Then he checked again. As a matter of fact, this project of "checking Harold's house" became an absorbing hobby every weekend that he could spare for the next several weeks. During Arthur's research, we uncovered a little more of the house's history. Evidently, one of the owners had been active in politics and often opened the house to conventions and rallies. We even found a guest book that included the signature of Eleanor Roosevelt.

One Friday Arthur arrived early and I was still at my office when he phoned me there.

"Harold," he said excitedly. "Do you care if I break a window?"

I was winding up an important meeting and it was only due to his manner and persistence that he had gotten through to me. Besides, I certainly did care. "Where?" I demanded. "What for?"

"There's a window painted black down in the basement at the back of the house. I've finally found about a six-foot discrepancy in my measurements between the outside and the inside of the basement. I'll have to break the window to see what's behind it. I'll pay for putting the glass back."

"Wait for me!" I ordered. "I'll be out in an hour."

Arthur and Carrol were waiting impatiently when I drove in. We went down into the basement where Arthur showed me a sketch he had made to scale and pointed to the blackened window, dirty and draped with cobwebs. From the basement floor it could only be reached by ladder, but it was only a little above ground level from the outside of the house.

"That's the culprit!" he announced. "I've got to see what's behind it!"

"What's so interesting about that? Can't you break it from the outside?"

"I don't want to," he replied impatiently. "The outside wall of the house runs in a straight line but down here the basement is all cut up into these rooms. There's about a six-foot space from that window to the outside wall or my figures are off—and they can't be!"

We pulled a ladder up to the window and Arthur climbed up with hammer in hand. Carrol and I stepped out of range of falling glass as he smashed the pane then, working with gloves, removed the remaining pieces from the frame. He turned his flashlight into the aperture and gave a sharp whistle.

"Hey!" he yelled. "You've got to see this! You won't believe it!"

He scrambled down the ladder and handed me his flash. Then he waited in obvious excitement for me to climb up.

"Do you see that room?" he shouted. "Look across at that other window!"

I saw it. The room was small and unfurnished although what looked like an old quilt was lying in one corner. Just opposite the window Arthur had broken was an identical one and this is what we had noticed from the outside of the house. It was, likewise, painted black and was a twin in its dimensions of the one in the basement wall. This was the most careful job of camouflaging a secret room that one could imagine.

Arthur's excitement was contagious. "There's another ladder around," I said. "Hand it up to me quick. I'm going down there!"

"I should be the one to go first," he protested.

"Nuts!" I replied. "I live here!"

Minutes later we both climbed down into our secret room. Careful examination proved that there were no other windows and no other way of getting into the room. If there had been a door, it was certainly sealed over with concrete. The entire room was cement lined. A patchwork quilt was on the floor in the corner. It was dirty and stained. There was also an old newspaper near it that I picked up, folded and put into my pocket. By working in teams, we found that hitting against the ceiling with a broom handle would give an answering vibration on the kitchen floor above.

We could only surmise that at one time there had been a trapdoor leading down from the kitchen to the hiding place. But a new floor had been laid, sealing it off completely. On top of this was linoleum which stretched from wall to wall. There was still no evidence of any exit from that basement room.

"Well, that's that," I observed. "Enoch was right. They did hide runaway slaves in this house. Evidently the operation became too dangerous and they sealed the room off with no chance for detection before they really ran into trouble. And Enoch probably had cleaned up blood on the kitchen floor from time to time if a slave had been badly beaten—or shot. There *must* have been a trapdoor leading down here from the original kitchen."

We left the room the way we found it.

When they arrived home that afternoon, Hal and Bob were as excited as the rest of us. As for Arthur, his enthusiasm and pride were boundless.

"I felt I'd find something," he crowed. "After all

these weeks, I was nearly ready to give up. But I was right all the time!"

"You're a good sleuth, Uncle Art," Hal admitted. "When I think of all the time I stood in the basement and looked at that window, I feel sort of stupid."

"No need to, Hal. No need at all," said Arthur graciously. "It took a lot of time and a lot of figuring to come up with the answer."

Enoch had been loitering in the kitchen even though it was now getting dark. He stepped to the dining room door. He was ready to leave.

"You got you a room, Boss. What good did it do?"

Enoch and I looked at each other with perfect understanding. "No good at all, Enoch," I answered. "The room is useless to us. Tomorrow we'll put the glass back and paint it over again like it was before. This was just a matter of satisfying a little curiosity."

He nodded, having accepted my curiosity as one of the facts of life for several months now.

After Enoch left, we still lingered over our coffee. It had been an exciting afternoon. Arthur was like a hound on a warm scent. "I'll bet these walls have a secret passage of some kind in them," he said.

I laughed. "Art, you've done a good job and you proved your point. But if you are going to do any digging or tearing down, I suggest you join an archeological expedition. We simply can't take this place apart. We don't even own it!"

He looked deflated.

Dorothy had been unusually quiet. Now she spoke thoughtfully. "Enoch is right, of course. What good does the secret room do? How does it answer what goes on in this house?"

Hal stared at his mother for a moment. Then he laid down his fork. "You're right, Mom. Even if someone could have gotten into that room without breaking the window, where would he have gone from there? He couldn't have gotten into the kitchen—not with three locks on the basement entrance."

Suddenly I remembered the newspaper and ran to get it from my coat pocket. "Let's take a look at this," I suggested. "Maybe it will tie in with some important event. I found it on the floor beside the old quilt."

They gathered around me as I spread it out, upsetting half a cup of coffee that Dorothy quickly sponged up. What I saw as I read that paper rocked me back on my heels—and I have never fully recovered. I couldn't speak. I could only point to the date. *The newspaper was only six months old.*

"My God!" gasped Arthur. "Someone *was* down there. They must have been reading by candlelight or something. It was only six months ago—and you were all here then!"

"You're right! We were here." I was completely baffled. "The kitchen floor is new, too! How did he get in?"

"How did he get through three locks," repeated Hal, remembering his experience in the kitchen, "and how did he get back into the room so quick if he was hiding?"

"The usual way, I presume," Dorothy replied serenely. "I can see no contradiction. It might be interesting to know if some of our guests missed a newspaper about six months ago."

"Now what are you getting at?" Arthur savagely ground out his cigarette.

"Just that I see no difference in transporting a newspaper down there into the basement room and in transporting a vase of spring flowers down the hall and into Mother's room," she replied calmly. "Especially spring flowers out of season—and in a snow storm."

"Do you mean to say that any ghost would be interested in reading a newspaper?" Arthur's face was flushed with irritation.

"I don't know the habits of ghosts," she replied. "But if it was taken with an intent to annoy, then I can accept that. A few of their habits I happen to be familiar with—not all."

"I won't buy that!"

"You don't have to. It's just my purchase." Her voice was still quiet and reflective. "I wonder if there was any pertinent news in that paper."

We checked it over carefully for any spectacular news, but it was simply the typical paper of the day. It did occur to me that the obituary column might offer a clue, but we knew none of the people listed there and no sensational local event was commented upon at all.

We never did figure out the answer to this enigma. So we had another mystery on our hands—one we never could solve.

Eventually Arthur was forced to relegate our ghostly manifestations to the same category as his UFOs. They seemed to be real, but they were unexplained—and likely to remain that way.

10

Drama in the Night

We had been in the house for more than a year, trying to establish a routine in between visitations, both psychic and corporeal. Many things had changed within the family—Michael exhibited the most obvious ones! Bypassing the crawling stage and shunning the playpen, our infant son was an infant no longer. He had boundless energy and ran—and climbed—all over the mansion, the yard, and the family.

The dogs served as nannies until we could hire someone. They watched over Michael, escorting him away from forbidden areas of the grounds, standing guard as cars drove in and out of the driveway, and generally keeping Michael as safe as was caninely possible. But Ching and Chang, as vigilant as they were, had limitations, and we continued our search for a fulltime, human nursemaid.

It was at this time that we found Clarabel. From North Carolina, she was separated from her husband

and had come to the Philadelphia area to look for work. When she came to us, she was penniless, helpless, and lost. I offered her the job—and free room and board. When she accepted, we were *all* very grateful!

We could always find Clarabel in the house. An avid snuff-dipper, she was constantly surrounded by the aroma of the snuff, and seemed to travel in a tobacco-scented cloud. Capable, warmhearted Clarabel adored Michael—and struck up a very close friendship with Hal and Bob, our two oldest boys. When she was not working, Clarabel was usually to be found sitting at the kitchen table, trading tall tales with the boys.

Clarabel stayed for three months. To my relief—and surprise—she was the only one of all our servants who had never been bothered by the spirits in the house. We were ready to settle down for a comfortable, steady time with Clarabel when she decided to leave. This time, we couldn't blame the mansion, the lady, or the footsteps. Her estranged husband had found her and convinced her to return home, to him and their marriage.

Six weeks after she left, we received a letter from Clarabel. The reconciliation was over. She said the marriage was finished—forever—and she wanted her old job back. We wired her traveling money and told her she was very welcome in the mansion. She came back almost immediately.

We were delighted. Clarabel very obviously wanted to stay with us for a while—and the spirits in the house seemed to have no objection to her being there. We thought we had finally solved our "help" problem.

Our relief was short-lived. No sooner had Clarabel resettled in her old room, when strange things began to happen. Footsteps would echo in her room. She'd turn on the light and find no one. Doors would open and close, with no one working them. She would feel the presence of people beside her, but never see them. Clarabel became upset and nervous. She felt that forces were being hostile to her; that she was the target for intense animosity—but she couldn't see who it was that hated her!

"They're after me!" she would wail, running for comfort to whoever was nearest. "They're out to get me! They follow me around all the time!"

We tried to console her. We assured her she was in no personal danger. She insisted that she was being persecuted. The trouble was that we couldn't prove, either to her or to ourselves, that she was mistaken.

One day Michael fell down the front steps and was badly bruised. He had no business being out there unsupervised and we questioned Clarabel about it. She burst into tears. "He was pushed, that's what! I saw it all! One minute he was standin' there and then he was pushed down them steps! It wasn't my fault!"

Dorothy and I were incredulous. Never had a physical attack been made on a member of the family and we could not believe that Michael would be singled out now. We reminded Clarabel that her only duty was to keep a constant check on Michael and she promised to be more careful.

The next incident happened a few days later. Michael climbed up on the railing of the veranda, no more than a few feet from the ground. Still, he fell off and broke his arm. When we returned from a trip to town, Dorothy and I found young Michael with his arm in a splint. A tearful Clarabel had summoned the doctor and things were under control. However, she was waiting on the porch with her bags packed.

"I'm leavin', Mr. Cameron," she sniffed. "They want me to leave. They are hurting Michael so you'll get mad and fire me. I really got to go!"

We tried reasoning with her, but it was useless. She was as adamant as our first servants had been and was determined to leave. So Clarabel left us; not sure why she was going—but convinced that she had to escape!

"Harold," Dorothy asked after Clarabel had left. "Do you really believe her story? Do you think that Michael was pushed down the steps and off that veranda railing?"

"No, I don't!" I replied emphatically.

"Neither do I. But what did happen? She was always so careful before."

"I think that Clarabel was so terrified that she was beside herself. I don't think she even knew where Michael was half the time. His accidents happened when we weren't around so she didn't have us to give moral support. She was probably hiding in a corner somewhere and was afraid to come out."

Dorothy gave a sigh of relief. "That's what I thought, too," she admitted. "I know that our lady wouldn't have had anything to do with an attack on Michael. Any kid can fall off a veranda railing if he's permitted to climb up on it. Even Hal fell out of a tree when he was little. I think these were all natural accidents."

I agreed.

"But there is one thing that I haven't been able to understand," she went on thoughtfully. "Why was Clarabel under psychic attack this time and not before?"

"I honestly don't know," I admitted. "It's bothered me, too."

* * *

With Clarabel gone, we were forced to depend on the chows again to supervise Michael when he got outside. They were full grown now and were both a blessing and a problem.

"I thought dogs were supposed to be psychic," Bob observed one afternoon after he had finished grooming Ching. "I've never known these chows to bark at anything except a real live person. And I know darned well that our lady has walked right by them because I heard her, myself, and I watched the dogs. Neither even flicked an ear."

"What about the time Carrol was camping out?" I reminded him. "They barked then."

Hal had joined us and was listening to the conversation. "That's right," he said reflectively. "Then they got plain scared. But that's the only time I remember, so I guess Bob has a point. Even Uncle Art was surprised when they didn't bark the first time he heard footsteps on the gravel."

"Maybe our lady likes dogs and they know it," Bob volunteered.

Their remarks set me off. "We really don't know much about animals except that they are supposed to have a sixth sense of some kind," I said. "Cats, for instance, are supposed to be the most psychic animals on earth. Maybe animals are born conscious of another world. Maybe they always sense things that we don't. And maybe they just don't feel that there is anything *new* to bark at. Perhaps they accept certain entities now just as they accept us."

"Well, they're pretty smart dogs," chuckled Bob, giving Ching a final pat of approval. "Maybe they don't want to waste the effort in trying to bite something that can't be bitten."

Hal laughed. "I wonder if you realize that one word

has been used this past year more than any other as far as we're concerned."

"What's that?" I asked.

"That little word, *maybe*."

I knew what he meant. "And maybe you're right," I told him.

Shortly after this talk, the chows' behavior changed abruptly.

It was well past midnight when I awoke to the sound of loud barking. I got up to see what the trouble was, thinking that a neighbor's horse had gotten loose and was coming down the driveway. Dorothy stirred in her sleep, but didn't wake up. I grabbed my robe and slippers, then went out, closing the door softly behind me.

The barking continued as I went downstairs and turned on the porch light. Then I went to the window to look outside. A woman was staggering up the path. The chows, strangely enough, were not nipping at her heels. They remained about five feet away and were backing up, shoulder to shoulder, every hair standing on end.

The strange procession continued until the dogs had backed up onto the front porch. I could see that the woman was wild-looking and disheveled, her hair hanging over her eyes. I hesitated about opening the door but I remembered the dogs were out there and that I could control them. At that moment she started to pound on the front door as she screamed, "Let me in! Let me in!"

I quickly left the window and opened the door. She fell into the front hall. The dogs had streaked in ahead of her, but still kept their distance, snarling viciously.

"Quiet!" I commanded. But the chows, usually so obedient, continued to snarl with hackles raised. They were like Siamese twins responding to a single impulse.

"It took a lot of courage to come past those dogs," I said. "Weren't you afraid?" I tried to sound casual, as if this sort of late-night visit was an ordinary occurrence.

"Dogs?" She barely glanced at them. "I'm not nearly as afraid of the dogs as I am of what's down there!" She pointed down the road toward the creek. I turned on an overhead light in the hall to get a good look at her. It took great control not to cry out.

She was wearing a black dress. It was on backwards and had been ripped in several places. It was obvious that she had nothing on beneath it. Her face was swollen and bruised. One eye was blackened and entirely closed. Blood had dried on the other cheek. Her hair was matted. She clutched the dress across her body as if to cover up as much of herself as she could.

I was horrified. "My God!" I cried. "What happened? Did you have a wreck?"

She laughed shrilly. "Wreck?" she echoed wildly. "I'm the wreck!"

I led the way to the kitchen where I had both brandy and coffee available. "I'll get my wife down here. She can help clean you up—lend you some clothes!"

"No! No! Don't bother her! I only want to use your phone."

"Who did this to you?"

"Two men."

"Where?"

"They've been holding me captive down at the creek. They both assaulted me!" Her voice rose on a hysterical note. "They assaulted me!"

"That's obvious. Where are they now?" I demanded.

Again she pointed. "Down there. Down at the creek.

They wouldn't let me go. They said if I tried to get away—if I screamed—they'd kill me sure!"

She wrung her hands and the folds of the dress, now released from her tight grasp, slid open to show a swollen and blackened thigh.

"I'll call the police!"

"No! I only want to go home. May I use that phone?"

"I'm calling the police," I insisted. "Men like that are dangerous. They should be picked up while they are still in the neighborhood!"

"No! Don't call them now!"

"How did you get away?" I asked. I wondered if the men could have followed her to the house and if I should run upstairs and get my gun. I also wished that the two boys were home in case I needed any help.

"They were drunk and I slipped away. They've been drinking for hours—empty bottles are all over the ground down there."

"Where?"

"Near the crossroads."

The crossroads were around the bend of the road and over a bridge about a quarter of a mile away. An old house was there—delapidated and fallen down, but some walls still leaned against the rotted wooden partitions.

"Did they keep you in the old house?" I asked.

"No. It was further on by the creek, but near there. They kidnapped me!"

I had put the coffee on to heat and I tested the pot. I felt she could use a strong cup of coffee. As a matter of fact, so could I.

"So you got away. Did they know?"

"Oh yes. But I got to the car and grabbed my dress. I hid in the ditch with the dress over me. It's black and they didn't see me.

"What did you do then?" I was trying to get a straight story. I still had every intention of calling the police.

"I ran. I saw the light in your upstairs window and I ran toward the light. I must use your phone!"

Her story rang true. The light she referred to was the night light in the nursery. She would have seen it after she came around the bend in the road.

"You sit there and drink your coffee," I commanded. "I'll call the police for you. You needn't talk any more just now."

"I won't talk to the police tonight!" she cried. I was amazed at the vehemence in her voice.

"Will you report it the first thing in the morning then?" I asked. "You owe that to other innocent people. These men have to be caught!"

"I think I know who they are," she replied impatiently. "I'll tell the police in the morning."

I looked at her more closely and shuddered. She had brutal bites and welts all over her neck and shoulders. "You've had a horrible time."

"They were horrible men!"

"You belong in a hospital. You should see a doctor."

"I belong at home. May I use your phone now?"

I led her to the phone in the hall. As upset as I was, I still looked over at the library door. It was closed.

"You don't need to phone," I said. "If you'll tell me where you live, I'll take you home."

"No. I'll call a cab."

"I'll call one for you," I offered, wondering if she were able to do it herself.

"No!" she cried angrily. "I can call!"

By this time I was exasperated. Never had the offers of a good Samaritan been refused so consistently and with such brusqueness.

"Suit yourself!" I replied shortly. I noticed that every

time the woman spoke, the dogs growled deep in their throats, but they did not approach her. I heard her order a cab and give our address. Then she hung up and we went back to the kitchen. There was no more conversation between us. She barely sipped at her coffee. About five minutes later I heard the cab drive up.

I walked to the door with her and motioned for the dogs to go out. They obeyed, but they were still growling, holding their tails as low to the ground as they could manage. I watched her stagger to the cab and climb in. No one got out to open the door for her. I called out to her, reminding her to report to the police the first thing in the morning or I would have to do it myself.

"I'll report it!" she yelled back over her shoulder.

I heard the noise of the engine as it was accelerated, and I heard the cab drive away. It was very dark and I didn't notice which company had sent the car. I patted the dogs who were still uneasy. Then I relocked the door and switched off the porch light. Finally, I wiped my forehead with the sleeve of my robe.

"Whew!" I said.

Upstairs, I woke Dorothy. "If I didn't know your real age," I told her when she looked at me sleepily, "I'd accuse you of sleeping through the San Francisco earthquake. It's my fault because I closed the door so as not to disturb you—but I sure could have used reinforcements. Didn't you hear the commotion at all?"

She sat up in bed. "I did hear the dogs—sort of," she admitted. "What was the trouble?"

"Oh, nothing much," I replied nonchalantly. "Just a woman. Just a case of kidnapping and assault and a half-crazy woman who wouldn't let me help her in any way or even call the police. She used our phone to call a cab."

Dorothy was wide awake by now and filled with concern. I thought, a little wildly, about the psychological blocks we all set up. She was tired and needed the rest, and slept through the noise downstairs. But if it had been a whimper from the nursery, she'd have been the first one there. I told her the whole story, admitting my own frustration and irritation at the strange visitor.

"But Harold," she protested, "you should have called me, anyway. That poor woman was in shock. She didn't know what she was doing!"

"Oh, yes she did!" I was still upset. "She knew exactly what she wanted to do and she did it. She also knew what she didn't want me to do—and I didn't do it. I should have called the police immediately and sent for a doctor. I still can't figure out how she talked me out of doing it! If I ever saw an apparition, she was it. But she did promise to report it in the morning!"

"I don't understand . . ." Her voice trailed off.

"Neither do I. What's the matter with this place?" I demanded, annoyed. "This whole area is nuts! Why can't things happen normally to us?"

"What was her name?" Dorothy wanted to know.

"She didn't bother to tell me. I should have gotten that, at least. But I didn't—I couldn't."

Neither did the police. When I phoned them early the next day, there had been no report made of the incident. I called at intervals during the day, making a pest of myself, but there was still no report. Then I called police stations in all the nearby towns and got the same negative results. I even checked with the police in Philadelphia. There was nothing on record. By this time I realized that the woman hadn't reported her attack to anyone—and had never intended to.

"Why not call the local cab company?" Dorothy suggested. "They'll know where their passenger was picked up and where she was taken."

"Of course!" I cried.

I phoned the cab company and learned that there had been no call at our neighborhood during the entire night. In desperation I called the cab companies in the surrounding towns. There was still no record of such a fare.

"That cab was here in about five minutes," I almost shouted. "It couldn't have come from too far away—even if it had been cruising—and what cab cruises around here after midnight?"

The boys were fascinated by my story. We went down to the crossroads. We looked through the old house—just in case. We searched along the creek for a quarter of a mile in both directions—and then for another quarter of a mile. There was no evidence of any drinking party—no bottles, no debris. There were also no tracks where a car might have been parked during those hours of the night that the woman had told me about.

"What about the ditch where she hid?" Hal asked at last.

That brought me up short. I swallowed hard. "Boys, we know this area," I managed to reply. "There isn't any ditch!"

They both regarded me strangely. "Are you sure it really happened, Dad? Could you have had a nightmare?" Hal sounded concerned.

I was too confused to be indignant. "What about the two cups of cold coffee on the breakfast table?" I asked. "And your mother heard the dogs."

"I wish we'd been home," said Hal.

"So do I," I replied fervently.

"Maybe this woman wasn't as innocent as she pretended to be," Hal volunteered. "Maybe she's a married woman in the neighborhood who let herself get picked up and doesn't want publicity."

"There's that word again," Bob said almost crossly. "Maybe . . . maybe . . . I'm getting sick of it. I'd like something clear-cut and definite for a change!"

"So would I," I retorted grimly. "Unfortunately life isn't always clear-cut and definite. But I think Hal's theory is the one the police have accepted—if they believe my story at all. But some of these pieces simply don't fit together. She was in a terrible state. I've never seen anyone as badly beaten up outside of a prize fight—and teeth are barred there. Then I heard her phone. I heard the cab drive up and watched it drive away."

"Did you ever know another family in your life to whom such strange things happen?" demanded Bob irately.

"I never did."

"And all since we've moved into this house," put in Hal thoughtfully.

We walked back to the house in silence. As with Ernestine's story of the reading lamp, something was nudging at my mind. I stopped.

"What's the matter, now?" Hal asked.

"I was just thinking about the dogs and the way they acted last night."

"Well, at least they barked," Bob remarked wryly.

"You know—it isn't the woman or the cab that bothers me now. It's those dogs—and it scares me."

"In what way?" Bob asked curiously.

"They were deadly afraid of her," I replied slowly. "They cringed on their bellies. They wouldn't come within five feet of her and they wouldn't stop snarling. They couldn't have been more terrified if she had come directly from hell!"

"Maybe she did," said Hal.

11

Enoch's Disclosures

I am not only persistently curious, I am also fairly stubborn. I continued checking the police stations for a couple of days in fruitless efforts to trace the midnight visitor. The strange woman was the topic of most of our family conversations for several days.

We had just gathered at the dinner table and Enoch was clearing up a few things in the kitchen before leaving for his tackroom. Winter was over and the days were getting longer, so our meals were planned accordingly. Enoch had never budged from his determination to leave the big house by dark. If we were late for dinner, he didn't even serve and Dorothy took over. He never objected to coming in the next morning and cleaning up any mess left in the kitchen as a result of midnight snacks or elaborate meals. He worked with a will in the early morning hours.

I had given him only a sketchy account of the midnight visit and he had shown the normal amount of interest, agreeing that it was odd that the police hadn't located the woman or picked up the two men who had so viciously attacked her.

"Maybe she was scared to tell on 'em," he volunteered. This attitude Enoch could understand. On the whole, however, the drama of the affair hadn't really seemed to bother him. Enoch could take physical happenings in stride. I hadn't mentioned the unusual reactions of the chows to him, either, thinking that it might make him uneasy.

"Just exactly where was this attack supposed to have taken place?" Dorothy asked on this particular evening.

"If it did take place—and it wasn't just another of our crazy happenings—it was down at the crossroads," I answered. "Somewhere along the creek just about a hundred yards from the old house, she said. But the boys and I searched the entire area and there was no evidence of anything there. The whole business is spooky."

We heard a crash in the kitchen. I went out to investigate, motioning for Dorothy to continue with her meal. I found Enoch standing motionless, staring at a shattered goblet on the kitchen floor.

"Don't worry about it, Enoch," I said, a little surprised. "We all break glasses."

He lifted his head and I was shocked at the sight of his face. It was the color of gray putty. He stared wordlessly at me for a moment and then dried his hands. I noticed that they were shaking.

"I gotta go now, Boss," he said desperately. "I don't feel so good." He took off his apron, reached for his coat, and stumbled out the door. "I'm sorry 'bout the glass," he mumbled as he left.

I stood there in amazement. Enoch had been pretty calm lately but right now he seemed terrified.

I looked down at the broken glass at my feet. He hadn't even attempted to pick it up so I went for a broom and dustpan. Enoch had received a shock—that was apparent. But from what? Had he been frightened by something in the kitchen? Had he heard footsteps or a rattle at the basement door? I went over and checked the locks. Everything seemed normal and the lights in the kitchen were bright. The dining room was only a few feet away and we were all there around the table. Had he overheard our conversation?

I went back in my mind to the words that had been said just before he dropped the goblet. It occurred to me then that I had never told Enoch just where the attack was supposed to have taken place and I remembered my words when I had described it in detail in answer to Dorothy's question. I had said: "down at the creek just past the old house." The creek, I told myself. The crossroads. The old house. These must have been the words that had so upset Enoch.

Right then I came to a decision. I was tired of being diplomatic with Enoch. I had spent most of his time with us catering to his superstitions. I knew that he *knew* the story of the mansion—that he probably knew who the lady was—and why she walked at night. But he would never talk about it—and I was getting desperate. Our lease would be terminated in three more months and then Enoch would be out of my life forever. I was going to get the truth from him now or I might never get it.

"What was the trouble?" Dorothy asked when I returned to the table.

"A broken glass," I said carelessly. I didn't add that I had to pick up the pieces after Enoch's flight.

I cornered Enoch the very next morning and asked to talk to him in the summerhouse. He started to mumble something about work to be done; I wouldn't listen to any excuses. I think he knew what was coming. We sat there in the sun and I wondered where to start. It was a beautiful morning—breezy and sunny —and we sat in silence. I glanced sideways at Enoch.

He didn't look well. He was still pasty-faced and his eyes, usually so dark and expressive, were lackluster. He seemed to be looking at something beyond me. I followed his gaze and saw that he was looking at the old tree.

"That's a magnificent maple, isn't it?" I asked, to begin our talk. "I've always admired it. I wonder how old it really is."

"Should have cut it down," he muttered tonelessly. "Cut it down an' burn it up good. Cain't figger why she never done it. Better'n the way she took, anyways."

"All right, Enoch," I said quietly. "Let's have it! Who is the 'she' you mention and what's the matter with the old tree?"

"It was there it happened . . . under the tree." His old hands were clenched. "The branches was like they is now . . . hasn't changed much . . . only the leaves was bigger." He was still muttering as if to himself.

"What happened? Was the doctor's wife hurt under the tree?"

He stiffened a little. "Her? No! 'Twas the young missy."

This was the first time that Enoch had mentioned a daughter. He had spoken of the doctor and his wife, but never of any children. I thought I understood.

"How old was the daughter, Enoch?"

He hesitated and I went on firmly. "You've got to tell me the whole story, you know. I've waited a long time. We'll be gone from here in only a few months. Then I won't bother you about all this. No more questions that upset you. You can keep as quiet as you want. But I want the story before we go. I want it now."

"I never even told Willie Mae," he answered slowly. "Don't seem fittin' somehow."

"Well, you can tell me. I'm entitled to know. I've gone through a lot of things in the old house. Besides, I'm your friend. I hope you know that by now."

He nodded slowly. "You is, at that. I really appreciate what you done for me." Then he sighed. "Might as well. It don't matter no more. It don't make no difference no more. I'm gettin' too old to care if I'm scared."

There was something terrible in his utter resignation, in his complete surrender. I took a deep breath. "Go ahead and talk, Enoch," I said quietly. "It might surprise you how much better you can feel when you let something out of your mind that has been bottled up for so long. I'll promise to keep quiet about it. I won't tell anyone."

He turned his head to look at me and I was surprised to see a glint of humor in his eyes. "Not even your wife, Boss?" he questioned.

"That's not fair," I protested. "Dorothy and I talk everything over. She's entitled to know, too. But she won't say anything. Not if I promise that she won't."

"It ain't that," he said in a halting manner. "You can tell 'er. But not 'til you leave. Not 'til you leave the big house for good."

I thought for a moment. "Okay," I agreed. "I give you my word. When we are finally out of the mansion, I'll tell her. Not before."

He gave a sigh of relief. "I jus' don't want 'er to know before," he confessed. "She's a mighty fine little lady. She's sweet an' she's kind. She likes black folks, too. I don't want to see her face after you tell."

I felt a prickle down my spine. I recalled Dorothy's

words spoken in the quiet of a night months ago. "Maybe we'd be better off not to know," she had whispered.

As Enoch still hesitated, I repeated my questions. "What happened to the girl? How old was she? What year was it?"

"Fourteen or fifteen, maybe. Her name was Lisa. She was so pretty, with them big blue eyes and yellow hair. Always laughin' and dancin' 'round. She loved the horses and spent a lotta time at the stables. She had quality, Boss, an' she knew it. She knew someday she'd be a great lady. She was bein' schooled for it— like a filly for the races."

The scene was being set. It was probably 1864 or thereabouts. Pennsylvania hardly counted as a Southern state, being above the Mason-Dixon line, but there were slave owners there and the southern traditions held in social life. Here was a pretty young girl who had reached the age where she must be taught how to conduct herself. She would learn the art of flirtation, the way to be nice to people but not let them get too familiar, the way to treat the blacks. In a couple more years she would be making her debut in a ball gown of pure silk with her hair piled up on her head. There would be music and dancing throughout the night. There would be damask tablecloths and silver, candlelight and champagne, with hurrying slaves carrying laden trays of food from room to room. I looked at the mansion and I could see it all—the beauty and grandeur of those past days. And there would soon be suitors from good families. This was the period that the Southern belle looked forward to the most and remembered the longest. I felt a stir of pity. Was Lisa never to know it?

"She minded pretty good," Enoch went on. "But sometimes she didn't."

"That's only natural in a child," I reminded him as he paused a little.

"She was like her mama in some ways. She had her own way of doin' things. But she liked everybody too much. She was awful nice to slaves, too. She'd rather be down with Ben and the horses than learnin' to sew an' pour tea without spillin'. So they sent her away to school in Atlanta." He sighed and shook his old head. "She came home for vacation. The first thing she done was make a beeline for the stables and her old pony."

Enoch stirred restlessly and ran a trembling hand through his hair. He was telling a graphic story. The girl had come alive for me. My eyes went to the stables that we had placed off-limits to the children. I could see them as they must have been once—clean and warm with the smells of hay and animals.

Enoch made a gesture across his face as if brushing off cobwebs. "She was more grown up, seems like, after she went to school. I saw the way Ben looked at her, but I still didn't pay it no real mind. Ben was a slave an' knew his place."

"Was Ben a groom?" I asked curiously.

"Ben?" Enoch looked at me. "He worked with horses, but he was the coachman. He lived in the coach house upstairs."

Again I felt the cold prickle. This couldn't be happening, I told myself. The pieces were beginning to fit. I looked around at the quiet yard that seemed to be basking in the morning sun. I smelled the perfume of roses. I heard birds singing. This story couldn't be happening ... but it was.

"Go on," I managed to say.

"It was a fox hunt. The doctor and his lady, they went ridin'. They was all excited and they looked mighty fine. Even the horses was keyed up and plungin' around. They always did that when a caper was comin' up. Lisa rode real good, but she didn't want to go. Her papa teased her 'bout rather readin' than ridin', but she said she'd got to study. Truth was, she tole me once she didn't like to see nuthin' killed."

The squeaky old voice broke for a moment and I realized what an ordeal this was for Enoch. But he went on resolutely. "Her folks was comin' by to pick her up for the dance later on. The missus said it was 'bout time that Lisa went—just to look on. But when they come back—she was gone."

"Gone?" I echoed. "Kidnapped?"

He shook his head. "I had to do an errand to that old house at the crossroads. It was pretty then. I had to get some salve for an ole pony that was sick. I was walkin' down the road and I looked back at the bend. Saw Ben goin' up the front steps. Thought 'twas funny he go up to the front door. Slaves always went to the back."

I nodded.

"I saw the door open and the little missy, she come out. She had dressed up for the dance early, I guess. It was a new dress . . . white with pink flowers an' a pink sash. She musta wanted to see how good she looked. She wuz studying in the liberry. They found her book on the sofa."

"How did he get her out of the house, do you think?"

"That'd be easy, Boss. She trusted the slaves. All he'd say was he wanted her to look at the pony. It was her pony what needed the salve."

"Did he take her back to the coach house?"

"Nope. He saw the tree and musta seen it was a good place. Nobody could see under them branches and everybody was gone anyways. The slaves was at the hunt or at another big house where the dance was goin' to be. All except the old cook and she was deaf and slept in the afternoons, anyways."

Enoch sighed deeply. One tear slid down his face. "I mighta stopped it if I'd gone back to see why Ben was at the front door. But I didn't. I just went on doin' what I was told. When I come back, it was all quiet. I didn't see Ben. I didn't ever fool with them horses so I left the salve and went in to clean up. The commotion started when the folks come home. They called and called and checked the neighbors to see if anyone knew where Lisa went. I tole them 'bout Ben goin' to the front door and her comin' out. Then they looked for Ben, too. They looked everywhere. Finally they looked—under the tree."

"Was Lisa there, Enoch?" I felt sick.

He shook his head. "Just her dress an' a pink dance shoe. The dress was torn a lot and had stains an' blood on it."

Enoch was talking stoically now as if nothing really mattered any more. "All the folks from the other houses come then. They had guns and dogs. They looked everywhere. They found her body in the creek that night—right past the old house. He musta hid her 'til later and then dumped her in the creek."

Enoch shook himself slightly. "Ben didn't think things out so good. Guess he just wanted her bad. After he did what he did under the tree, he knew he had to kill 'er. Anyway, that's what he said when they ketched him."

"What happened to him, Enoch?"

"The slaves hung him," he replied grimly. "They didn't even wait for her papa. They said no use him gettin' his hands dirty on scum!"

We sat in silence for several moments. "So," I mused aloud. "It's the little missy who walks the house—who comes from the library and climbs the stairs."

Enoch straightened. "Not her, Boss. She's walkin' them golden streets in heaven and playin' a golden harp. It's the lady, that's what!" Again he shivered.

"Oh!" I should have known that there was a brutal ending to such a horrible story of rape, murder and lynching. "What happened to her, Enoch? She must have nearly gone crazy."

"Not wild crazy," he replied thoughtfully. "Just quiet crazy. She went 'round like nuthin' happened after the funeral. I heard her hummin' when she trimmed the roses. It was just when she looked at you with them eyes that you felt funny. All the time she acted like she just heard a big noise an' wondered if to run. All the time you kept thinkin' maybe she'd scream— but she nevah did."

I thought that Enoch had done very well in describing a woman under unbearable tension. He went on soberly. "She spent more'n more time in the liberry. One day she didn't get herself dressed at all . . . just had on a fancy night gown and a robe and slippers with no backs to 'em. She had tea in the liberry and then when I took out the tray she reminded me to keep the room dusted good.

"'Always keep it dusted and shining, Enoch,' she said to me. 'Lisa loved this room . . . she read for hours in here.'

"I was sorta upset 'cause I'd worked hard in there that very mornin' but she didn't seem to know it. I took the tea things out and washed up the cup. I 'member puttin' the cream back and the sugar. Funny I think of them things now."

"Go on, Enoch."

"After I left the liberry, she just climbed the stairs to the top floor, Boss. I don't know where she got the rope. She hung herself out of that big window in front."

He pointed toward the house with a shaky finger.

"You can't see that window from here, Enoch," I said faintly.

"I can see it from anywhere," he replied stonily. "She just hung there . . . movin' from side to side, real slow. I saw 'er."

Enoch's story was nearly over. He sat, a huddled heap of misery. "I ain't done what she said. I ain't nevah dusted the liberry. I been scared to meet her, Boss. Them eyes . . . they strike me dead!"

I reached over and put my hand on his. "Thanks for telling me, Enoch," I said gently. "I knew that something violent had happened here. Now I know who to pray for. Our lady still walks the halls but she won't hurt anyone except herself. She can't forget yet—and neither can the coachman. Aren't you afraid of him, too?"

" 'Course I is . . . but not so much. I never seen him later. I just heard that he didn't fight none. When he seen the rope, he wanted 'em to do it."

"Well, you just pray that God will help them both. There's nothing else you can do. It was a long time ago."

He bowed his head. "God rest their souls," he said. Then, as if the words startled him, he looked around at me. "Funny, Boss. I been a good Christian and I know my Bible. How come I nevah thought to pray for them souls before?"

"Because you've spent all your time in the Old Testament, Enoch. You know it well, but I've never heard you quote Jesus and he gave us a new idea of God. He preached a loving Father that could understand and forgive. He told us about the law of love. We are to forgive our enemies and those who have done evil—and to pray for them, too."

He thought this over doubtfully.

"And God rest your *soul*, Enoch. You don't have to carry this burden any longer by yourself. You can give it up. Give up your hate and your fear and your grief. Give it to God. And ask him to take care of your memories, too."

"I guess you're right," he said with a deep, shuddering sigh.

I rose to my feet. "Better take the day off, Enoch. Get yourself a bottle if you want to. Try and forget. Go preach a sermon down in the orchard."

He looked at me, startled.

"Oh, I've heard you preach Enoch. You are a mighty fine preacher—a mighty fine preacher, indeed."

He got up slowly and looked for a long time at the maple tree. Then he spoke huskily. "Thank you, Boss."

I watched him amble away with his rolling, lopsided gait, and smiled wryly. It occurred to me that I had prescribed two antidotes for Enoch's condition—prayer and gin. Most churches would consider them to be quite contradictory. But I felt the need for both antidotes, myself.

I walked slowly up to the house and it seemed that I was following other heavy footsteps up the graveled path—purposeful steps, driven by an evil impulse that could not be withstood. I jerked myself back to the present just in time to keep from walking around to the front porch. I swerved sharply to the kitchen door.

Inside there were dishes in the sink awaiting Enoch's attention. On an impulse I put on Dorothy's apron, much too small for me, and started cleaning up.

"What do you think you're doing?"

Dorothy stood behind me with laughter in her eyes while Michael straddled one hip. He was wiggling in protest at being taken on one of his frequent trips to the bathroom for clean clothes and a face-washing.

"Where's Enoch?" she questioned. "I saw you talking to him down there."

"Enoch isn't feeling too well today. I told him to take some time off and rest up." I didn't mention the bottle that I'd also suggested.

She was immediately concerned. "What's the matter with him, Harold?"

"Just old age, hon. He says he's getting too old to care any more."

I only spoke the truth. Dorothy's eyes softened. "Poor Enoch," she said. "He's been such a Godsend to me. I hope he takes all the time he needs. But you needn't do the dishes. I'll take care of the kitchen."

"Not this morning, you don't. I don't go to the office until afternoon."

"Since when?" she demanded.

I grinned at her. "Since right now. Take care of your son. I'll straighten up here!"

It proved easier to keep my promise to Enoch than I had anticipated. I didn't find myself bursting to spread his news. I would watch Dorothy's face, soft with love, as she buttoned up Janet's dresses and tied a gay bow in the smoothly brushed hair. I listened to her laughter when she and her young daughter shared an amusing secret. I saw her kneel at Janet's bed while the child said her prayers and reached up her arms for a hug and a goodnight kiss.

How wise old Enoch had been, I thought more than once. It was much better that she did not know.

12
Enoch Disappears

Enoch's final and reluctant disclosures spurred me to action. I checked the calendar. Our lease had less than three months to run. The last month was already paid for and I could forfeit the free month's rent covered by the initial deposit if I so desired—and I so desired! If I could now find another, suitable, house to rent, I knew I could afford to forfeit the money and terminate the lease on the mansion. I knew only one thing: *I wanted to be out of that house!*

Although moving would entail a great amount of work and six weeks or so wasn't giving me too much time to find other quarters, I got busy. I was by now firmly entrenched in my new position. I also had contacts with many more people. In addition to the realtors, I enlisted the help of my office staff and business associates in Philadelphia.

"I want a suitable home," I informed them. "But

not in the area of Wynne, Darby, Lansdowne, Ridley Park, Chester—or any town near them!"

"Ye Gods!" one of the secretaries laughed. "What you really mean is that you want a place out of Philadelphia, but in an opposite direction from where you are now!"

"That's it," I agreed.

My luck seemed to be changing. In a few weeks I found an attractive colonial home in the Valley Forge area, some thirty miles west of Philadelphia. It was another old home, to be sure, but not nearly as old as the mansion and it was equally as well constructed. I drove Dorothy over to look at it and she immediately approved. It didn't have a new and sparkling kitchen, but it was sturdy, clean, and in excellent condition. We could do any needed repairs when we were settled in. I signed a lease immediately, but this one I read carefully!

By now our circumstances were a little different, too. The family seemed to be shrinking. Almost without warning Hal had gone into the Army and Bob, not to be outdone, was being trained as a Navy pilot.

"This is a nice house and plenty big enough now that the boys are away," Dorothy assured me contentedly. "It will be so nice to feel cozy in a house for a change."

"It will, indeed," I agreed wholeheartedly. "We can now start packing a few things at a time. We'll store the boxes in the basement or take them over to the new place in the station wagon. And we'll also take everything in the wagon that we don't want to trust to a moving van."

Valley Forge was only about forty-five miles away from Media. The rolling hills were green and beautiful and the homes in the area attractive. Even the battlefields and former encampments, now a national monument, were peaceful. We toured it one afternoon and it was hard to visualize the violence and anguish that had once characterized the area. I was reminded of some lines in a poem by James Russell Lowell:

> "Who knows whither the clouds have fled?
> In the unscarred heavens they leave no wake;
> And the eyes forget the tears they have shed,
> And the heart forgets its sorrow and ache.
> And the sulphurous rifts of passion and woe
> Lie deep in a silence pure and smooth,
> Like a burned-out crater, healed with snow."

The atmosphere surrounding the new home was going to be quite a contrast to that of the mansion.

Enoch was tired. He had saved some money, I was sure, and I felt he was looking forward to retiring when we moved away. But I also knew he would serve us faithfully as long as we needed him. When we took on the added chores of sorting and packing the things we needed, and discarding those we did not want, Enoch continued to be invaluable to us. We gave him many items that he said he could use. It was a surprise, therefore, when he didn't show up for work one morning.

I opened the kitchen door, but there was no Enoch. We waited for him to arrive to prepare breakfast, but no Enoch. Finally Dorothy came down to scramble eggs and slice ham. I hoped that Enoch wasn't ill, and I fully expected him to be on the job when I got home from work.

"Enoch didn't show up all day," Dorothy greeted

me. "Don't you think you had better check on him while I finish getting dinner? He must be ill."

I went down to Enoch's tackroom and found everything in order. No one else was living in the barn just then. Enoch's companions, the prisoners, had long since completed their work-release program. Everything was quiet. There was no one to ask about Enoch. Butch had been sleeping outside the closed door of the tackroom, his massive head on his paws, but he woke and thumped his tail in greeting. Enoch used to leave Butch on guard when he was away and Butch was faithfully at his post. There was no sign of his master. If Enoch had been stricken, it had happened somewhere away from home. I took Butch back to the house and fed him a good meal. Then he trotted back toward the barn. He was waiting for Enoch, too.

When Enoch still hadn't appeared by the next morning, I resolved to start a search for him as soon as I got home that night. I was going to have to be out of town for several days and I didn't like to leave Dorothy in the uncertain situation of not knowing when Enoch would be returning to help out with the chores.

That night, after finding that Enoch was still missing, I drove down the road to call on Willie Mae. There was the chance that he had been taken ill while calling on her and that she would be taking care of him in the servants' quarters at the imposing residence where she lived. It was unlike Enoch not to get word to us but Willie Mae might have promised to do so and had forgotten.

I sat in the car and looked at the house, remembering the first time I had driven Enoch down to see his girl friend. I, too, went to the back door.

Willie Mae listened impassively when I told her

that Enoch hadn't shown up for work for two days and that I was worried about him. Then she gave a toss of her head.

"Lawdy, Mr. Cameron! Didn't you know that Enoch was goin' to Atlantic City?"

I was stunned. "I certainly didn't know it! He never mentioned it to me. He didn't even wait for payday."

"Oh, he never tells folks when he goes off like this," she said airily.

"You mean he's done it before?" I was still incredulous.

"Lots of times. You don't know Enoch so well, do you, Mr. Cameron—even if you are his boss. Sometimes he's gone for weeks at a time. He just gets an itchy foot and takes off."

I was still amazed. "You aren't worried?" I demanded.

"Who, me?" She giggled in a high register that was particularly irritating. "Enoch can take care of hisself. He'll be back one of these mornings. He'll be over for flapjacks and molasses. Don't you worry none 'bout Enoch." She half turned away. "I'm right busy, Mr. Cameron. I've got my own work to do now."

"I'm sorry to have bothered you," I said stiffly. "If you hear from Enoch, will you phone me?"

"That I will," she promised unconcernedly. "Might get a postcard any day. He always sends me one from wherever he's at—sooner or later, that is."

"I didn't think he could write," I said.

She hesitated and something flickered in her eyes. "He can write *my* name, Mr. Cameron. The mails, they do the rest."

I still lingered. "You don't think that he might have had a little too much to drink—and have gotten into trouble?"

Her dark eyes narrowed, but she replied in a casual voice. "Not Enoch. He's been 'round. Much longer than you have—or me, either. He can take care of hisself." With that she closed the door.

Fuming to myself, I drove back to the house to talk the visit over with Dorothy.

"That's strange," she observed. "I would have thought that Enoch hadn't traveled over ten miles or so from home in his entire life."

"Well . . . maybe he goes on these sprees and that gets him started. People do funny things under the influence of alcohol."

"Maybe," she agreed, but her voice was doubtful.

"What's bothering you?"

"Nothing I can put my finger on," she confessed reluctantly. "It's just that I thought I really knew Enoch. It isn't like him to just disappear like this. He knew I was depending on him. And to go to Atlantic City of all places! What's in Atlantic City for a man like Enoch?"

I shook my head. "As I said, people do odd things, sometimes. We'll just play it by ear and see what happens."

"There isn't much else that we can do," she replied with a little frown.

I was unusually busy just then. My few days out of town stretched to two weeks with a flying visit to Canada. My only contact with the family was by phone. When I returned and there was still no word from Enoch, I decided to do something else about trying to locate him. I crossed Willie Mae off my list. I didn't trust her. If she had really cared for Enoch, she would have shown a little more concern. I went to the police station and told them my problem. The lieutenant at the desk consulted his blotter.

"A black?" he asked absently, thumbing through some records.

"Yes. Very old. He's quite small and thin."

He came to an entry and read it through silently. Then he looked up at me. "Would he have been an old man wearing blue pants and a white shirt?"

"That's the one. Was he picked up for something? Is he in jail?"

"He was picked up for being dead," came the somber answer.

I felt as though he'd hit me in the stomach. "Dead? When? Where? Was he hit by a car?"

"Don't know for sure how long he'd been dead. But it was several days when he was found by a couple of boys who were hunting woodchucks. His head was bashed in by a two-by-four. Hit from the back. Death must have been instantaneous. He didn't know what happened."

"Where was he found?"

"In one of those steep gulleys back of an old barn. Past the crossroads."

So it had been fairly close to home. "Why wasn't I notified?"

"We didn't know about your connection with him. He had no identification and no relatives, evidently. No one claimed the body. He was buried in Potter's Field."

"No one came forward at all?"

"Not that we have any record of. Somebody might have come out of curiosity. No relatives or friends, though." He closed the book. "Sorry, Mr. Cameron, but we just didn't have anything to go on. As I say, we didn't know he was working for you."

"Hadn't anyone reported him missing?"

"Not until now." The case was closed as far as the

lieutenant was concerned and I got the unspoken message. What was one old black man to him? Especially one with no family and no identification? Yes, the case was most definitely closed.

There was no point in asking if they had found any money on him. Even if he had been carrying around some of his hard-earned wages, whoever had struck him down must have gone through the pockets. I got to my feet and thanked him for his trouble. Then I drove back home and broke the bad news to Dorothy. She turned very white and then started to cry.

"I'm sorry," she whispered at last. "So very sorry. You say he was hit in the back of the head. That means he was murdered?"

"Evidently. His head was bashed in, according to the police. They have closed the case. They had nothing to go on then—even less by now."

"But why?" she cried passionately. "Why? He had no money on him—at least I don't think he did. He wasn't in the habit of carrying money around—and it wasn't payday yet. Why would anyone kill a dear old man like Enoch? He didn't deserve an end like this!"

I was busy with my own black thoughts. "He did have an insurance policy," I reminded her grimly.

She stared in dismay. "Oh! Then you think . . ."

"I don't know what I think," I retorted angrily. "But maybe Enoch was taking too long to just die a natural death. I'm going to have another talk with Willie Mae."

There was no masking her unfriendliness at this second visit and I didn't try to camouflage my own feelings, either. I didn't like the woman and I didn't care who knew it.

"You lied about Enoch!" I accused. "You knew he didn't go to Atlantic City. Why did you lie? If you'd told me the truth, I'd have gone to the police then. Maybe we could have found him in time to save his life!"

"He was already dead by then," she said with a shrug. "What good it do?"

"Did you know he was dead then?" I demanded.

" 'Course not."

"But you do now," I accused her hotly.

"I hear things," she retorted coldly. "Besides you just told me, yourself."

As I stood there looking at her in disgust, she burst out angrily, "I didn't think it was any business of white folks, anyhow!"

"Enoch was my business. I liked him. He worked for me. Evidently I liked him a lot more than you did," I remarked savagely.

Her lips tightened, but she said nothing. I thought about mentioning the insurance policies, but decided not to. I couldn't prove that there was an insurance policy. I only had Enoch's word for it and, while I knew Enoch had never lied to me, I couldn't prove that the policy was still in effect, either. I didn't even know the name of the insurance company nor of the investigator. It was a cinch I wasn't going to get any information out of Willie Mae. By this time there were other hostile black faces behind her in the kitchen. I turned on my heel and went back to the car.

The next morning, however, I went back to the police and told them about the insurance policy. They, of course, asked me the name of the company. I couldn't give it to them and I couldn't prove that the premiums had been paid to keep it in effect. I gave them Willie Mae's name, but the lieutenant only shook his head again and this time it was a decided shake. An investigation would be a lot of trouble—and for what?

So, Enoch's story was over.

* * *

Now that we knew what had actually happened to our old servant, the place seemed even more depressing and empty. Both Dorothy and I prayed that he would be taken care of now. I went down to the clearing where he had preached so many of his sermons and looked up at the trees. It seemed ironic that the danger he had sensed in the area all his life had finally caught up with him just when he seemed to have come to terms with it. I felt rebellious and then I remembered the advice I had given him such a short time ago about giving the anger and hate and fear to God.

"I'm sorry, Enoch," I said aloud. "Sorry this had to happen. But you have nothing to fear any longer. Remember the Bible . . . remember your mother . . . remember your faith. Turn to God wherever you are and follow the light. You'll be all right with Him and I know your mother is close by."

When I turned back to the house I told myself that I, too, was going to have to hold on to my own faith and get rid of my feelings of resentment and fury.

Dorothy was sensitive to my moods. She didn't ask where I had been; perhaps she knew. She laid a comforting hand on my arm.

"It was a senseless crime, Harold. But we didn't know. We couldn't have done anything about it. He must have been killed that last night after work."

"He said this place wasn't anything but trouble," I replied grimly. "He feared the mansion all his life, but couldn't get away. He had no place to go. He had no friends. There was no one to turn to but us."

"Don't torture yourself," she pleaded. "It would have been too late even if we had found him that first morning he didn't show up."

"I sometimes wonder . . ." I broke off.

"I know what you wonder," she said swiftly. "You are wondering if the mansion is somehow to blame—if his death was the result of an attack by the unseen forces he was so afraid of."

I nodded.

"I don't believe that," she said positively. "I think what happened to Enoch originated right here on this physical plane in some greedy, malicious mind and that it would have happened regardless of the mansion . . . regardless of our experiences here."

I sighed. "That's what I really want to think," I admitted. "But as we have felt so often, there is a dark cloud over this place. I'll be glad to get away—and we're going to speed things up, too."

13

Moving Day

The next three weeks dragged on in spite of the fact that we were busy trying to do all the work ourselves. We still heard footsteps, we still saw knobs turning, we still had visits in the night. But we ignored them all. We were used to them by now. And we would soon be leaving them all behind. I took time off from the office, when I could, to lend a hand. Moving day came at last. Bob wasn't able to get home on leave, but Hal made it back for the weekend. The family was almost together.

The furniture was finally on its way to Valley Forge by midafternoon. We left a few hours later. Hal was driving the station wagon, which was loaded to the top. Janet and Carrol were with him in the front seat. Dorothy and I were to follow in the family car with Michael asleep in the back. He had missed his nap in the confusion of loading and packing and was now sleeping on a pile of extra blankets and pillows, shored up by packing boxes.

I made a final check of the house. As usual, I saw that all the doors were triple-locked from the inside, including the door from the kitchen to the basement. I addressed and stamped a letter to Brooks, the real estate agent, and enclosed all the keys to the house after I locked the front door from the outside. I intended to drop the letter into the first mailbox we passed going through town.

After we turned out of the driveway, I knew I had one final job to do. I drove to the bend in the road just on the other side of the creek from where we had first glimpsed the mansion. Then I parked the car and turned off the motor.

Dorothy looked a little surprised, but accepted the pause. Together we gazed back at the imposing old residence. It was nearly the same time of day as it had been the first time we saw the mansion. I stared at the building . . . at the chimneys that thrust themselves up into the darkening sky. I looked long and hard at a certain window on the third floor—a window that I had refrained from looking up at during the past few weeks. Then I put my arm around Dorothy's shoulders.

"Sorry to be leaving?" I asked.

She gave a violent shake of her head. "Any woman is happy where her family is, but aside from that, I don't think I was ever really happy in that house. I don't know why exactly. Nothing too bad ever happened to us—except losing Enoch. We were never hurt. We had some good times. But there was something else. You said once that it was a dark cloud and that's the best way I can describe it, too. It was almost a feeling of doom. I can't explain it exactly but you know what I mean."

"Yes, I know," I replied quietly. "I have something to tell you, honey. I've known it for a little while but I promised Enoch I wouldn't tell you until we were out of the place for good. Then, I want you to forget it. But it will explain the cloud."

There, in the gathering twilight, I told her the tragic and heartbreaking story of the mansion. I told her of the fox hunt and the dance that was canceled. I told her of the rape, murder, and suicide. I told of our lady who climbed the stairs to a room on the third floor one day on a grim errand of her own; of the coachman who walked purposefully to the front door and waited for a pretty young girl to answer the knocker. And I told her about the strangled little body being recovered from the creek down past the old house only a few hundred yards from where we were sitting.

As I talked, I could feel her stiffen with shock. Then I felt the trembling start beneath my hand. I wasn't surprised when she wept.

"H-how t-terrible," she faltered at last. "Oh, God, how terrible! A little girl . . . still a little girl when it happened. That poor mother! How could she stand it?"

"She didn't," I reminded her gently. "She couldn't."

I gave her plenty of time to compose herself and finally she wiped her eyes with a tissue she had drawn from her purse with trembling fingers.

"Oh, Harold," she moaned. "I've admired that maple and I was sure she did, too. I've climbed those same stairs she climbed that awful day! I've been in her library and dusted some of the same old books. I've sat in her summerhouse and admired the roses, too. It's as if these years had telescoped somehow and I could reach out and touch her. She is so real to me, so poignantly real!"

I patted her shoulder. "I know. She's real to me, too." I thought of those last days of strain that Enoch had described so vividly—of those eyes of which he was so terrified—of the agony that had motivated her last action of protest.

"But it's different with me," Dorothy cried. "She's my sister because I'm a woman, too; a woman with children I love and pray for. What hurt her then hurts me now. Time seems to be unimportant. I've never really appreciated this sense of unity with all humanity before. It's as if we suffer and rejoice and rise and fall together!"

I could only nod in silent agreement.

"Tell me," she went on urgently, "could we have helped her if we had known? Could we have talked to her—have helped to free her from the endless activity—that despairing cycle?"

"I don't know," I replied honestly. "Before we moved into the mansion, I never had the faintest idea that things like this could happen. I've learned a lot—and I intend to learn a lot more. I know something, though. I'm not leaving the mansion the same man that I was when we moved in."

Dorothy sighed. Suddenly she cried out, "I want to drive away and never look back!"

I started the motor. "We're going to do just that," I assured her.

Logically, that should have been the end of the story. But logic had never been characteristic of happenings in the mansion. I stopped in Wynne, and dropped the envelope with the keys at the post office. Brooks would get it in the morning mail. The gesture was my last tie with the mansion. From that moment on it belonged to the past.

We drove on to the new house at Valley Forge. All the lights were on in welcome. The youngsters were waiting impatiently for our arrival. They were hungry and I had promised to take them out to dinner. The moving van, partially unloaded, was parked in the driveway with the final unloading to be done the next morning under Dorothy's supervision.

Brooks called me at the office the next day. He was angry and sounded upset.

"I didn't think you'd pull a trick like that, Mr. Cameron! I really didn't! The place could have been cleaned out overnight! If I hadn't driven over to look around, I don't know what might have happened!"

"What are you talking about?" I demanded.

"We've had our differences," he went on angrily, "but this was a pretty cheap trick. You had no right to go off and leave the place open like that!"

"Open?" I echoed incredulously.

"That's what I said."

"But I didn't," I protested swiftly. "I locked everything up and mailed you the keys. Didn't you get them?"

"I did. That's the reason I went over. I knew you people were finally out. But what do you mean you locked up? Every door in the place was standing wide open!"

It took me a full minute to understand him.

"Well?" he prompted when I didn't speak. "I'd like an explanation!"

I thought of certain conversations I'd had with the indignant Mr. Brooks—conversations where I had been at a distinct disadvantage. I had waited a long time for this and I was savoring it. I laughed aloud.

"Okay, Brooks," I said. "I always had the feeling you didn't believe me when I tried to get out of that lease. So you listen now—and you listen well. I put new locks on every door. There are no extra keys floating around, either. You have them all. I locked the house and I left it locked!"

"B-but then h-how . . ." he stuttered.

I ignored him. "If you found every door wide open this morning, it wasn't done by human hands. Now it seems that you have a little problem of your own. I hope you can keep the place locked. At least that's one area where we had no trouble. I wish you luck in renting that place," I added cheerfully, "and in keeping it rented. As for me and my family, we're through with all the problems connected with the mansion—now and forever!"

I hung up the phone on a dead silence at the other end of the line—a silence broken only once by a startled gasp.

At dinner that night I gleefully reported the conversation for I was human enough to get a certain satisfaction out of Brooks's discomfiture. The dining room was cheerful and a fire was burning on the hearth. After only a few hours, the house felt like home.

"I wonder if you spoke the truth," Dorothy mused. "Are we really free from all the problems posed by that house?"

"Probably not," I admitted. "But from now on they are in the mental, speculative area and I hope to have some answers to them before I die."

I had taken Hal aside earlier and told him of Enoch's disclosures and we agreed the less discussion of the tragic details of those long-ago events in Dorothy's presence, the better. Now he spoke thoughtfully.

"You know, Dad, I've felt for a long time that there might be more of them around than just the lady and the coachman. You always said that our case would be a weak one in court, but we know we have witnesses to everything that did happen except one incident that still bothers me."

"And I know what that is," I said quickly. "It's my midnight visitor—that crazy woman!"

"Right! It seems so out of context when you think of everything else that went on and it doesn't fit into any category that ties in. There's no one to corroborate your story except that Mom remembered the barking of the chows that night and that you went downstairs. The only evidence was the two cups on the breakfast table the next morning. But how strong is our evidence that this was another case of a psychic phenomenon?"

"Not strong at all," I replied promptly. "You'll remember that I was so sure it was an entirely physical event that I contacted the police and the cab companies. I saw the woman and I spoke to her, but I never touched her at all. I saw the cab and heard the motor but, again, I didn't go out to open the door for her or to talk to the driver. It wasn't until later that things didn't add up—the strange behavior of the dogs that was entirely out of character, our fruitless search for the site of the drinking spree she had described, no record of a cab even being in the vicinity and the absence of any police report. These are mystifying, but I admit if it hadn't been for the other strange things that had happened in and around the mansion, I wouldn't have felt that it might be a psychic happening."

"Could it be that time as we know it isn't really relevant? Could it have been something that happened at a different time and place entirely?"

"It would have had to be later," I reminded him. "Telephones and cabs—they don't belong a hundred years or so ago."

"Well, we have facts enough for the rest, that's for

sure. But have we any answers that cover *every-thing?*"

"Merely speculative ones. But suppose there is a magnetic, psychic atmosphere around that old mansion that could be compared to a piece of sticky fly paper. The paper wouldn't discriminate as to the kind of flies or insects it attracted, would it? A magnet wouldn't attract a certain thumbtack or a specified nail. There were so many tragic events connected with the mansion—the fire and death of several people living in that house, the runaway slaves, some of whom may have died there; the other tragedies . . . All of that must be taken into consideration when we postulate a theory of a powerful magnetic field in that specific area."

We were silent for a moment, each busy with our own thoughts. Suddenly Hal grinned. "No matter how many there might have been," he observed, "it looks as if they had the last word, doesn't it?"

I agreed with a rueful smile. "Well, I can't think of a better way of telling us that the house on Plum Tree Lane needed a good airing out!"

Epilogue

Many years have passed since our two-year residence in the house on Plum Tree Lane.

Our children have grown, married, moved away. Bob died unexpectedly of a heart attack while still young. Dorothy, my loving wife, died a few years ago. I have since remarried.

I retired from my business career and moved back to the West Coast. Spurred by my personal experiences with psychic phenomena which could not be explained by logic, rational reasoning or even materialistic science, I turned to the study of metaphysics.

I am now the pastor of a Religious Science Church in Paradise, California. I always meant to write my own personal "ghost story," but never started it until I met Connie Westbie, who just happened to be a member of my congregation. (Another psychic coincidence?) Together we set down this story. *Night*

Stalks the Mansion is a true account of what happened in a haunted house.

What started in Wynne—my sensitivity to psychic phenomena—seems to have continued since then. I'm not sure why. Perhaps because I am more aware of other dimensions—and my consciousness has been raised.

Two such psychic experiences stand out. Once, after Dorothy died, I was preaching a sermon at my church on Sunday. After the service, one of my congregants asked who the woman was who sat in a chair on the platform during my sermon. I hadn't seen a woman, but the congregant insisted she had. I asked for details; she described Dorothy! She had never met my wife, but was able to depict Dorothy's face and appearance, even down to her dress, an old-fashioned favorite that Dorothy had worn years ago!

The other incident was just as inspiring as the first. I had received the news of Bob's death, all the more shocking because it was so unexpected. I was in my study, preparing myself for the two different sermons I was to give later that day. I stood at my desk and decided that I didn't have the strength to face my congregations. I looked up and there was Bob! He was smiling at me, and I remember noticing that his front teeth, which had been broken and repaired, were now perfect. He gave me a sign, one that seemed to say, "Hang in there. You can do it." So I did.

Everyone in the family who was conscious of the lady on the stairs and the coachman on the path felt touched in some way by them. My son Harold, questioned a few years ago, still remembers the experiences vividly:

"The strange events at the house on Plum Tree Lane are as unexplainable to me now as when they happened some thirty years ago.

"I remember Enoch saying, 'Yes, boys, there are two ghosts in the old house—that's why I always leave before dark. But don't worry. Old Missus is a good ghost and will never hurt you. The other one has done all the harm he ever will—and he won't hurt you now, either.'

"Enoch had been right. We spent almost two years with those two earthbound souls, but they never hurt anyone in the family. After the first six months, we even came to appreciate our unique experience.

"I am my father's oldest son, nearing sixty, but the memories of the days when, as a college boy, I lived in that house on Plum Tree Lane, are as vivid and mystifying now as then. They remain the most exciting and memorable days of my life."

Carrol was only ten when we moved to the mansion, but has assured me that he will never forget the two years we spent there:

"I was really too young to appreciate the beauty that the mansion held for me, although I did believe that we became 'special people' as a result of living there. The old house held a presence of history and I was aware of the stories it could tell. This awareness seemed to be a constant companion as I walked through the halls and the various rooms. But what I remember most clearly was my constant fear at being there, for I knew that the house was master and holder of many secrets that I'd just as well not know. I would like the mansion to know that during our brief time there, I was carrying a white flag of truce.

"Living with the 'Grand Dame' in the house was a rewarding experience. Like the sea, it was beautiful, but you learned to beware."

Janet and Michael were too young to carry any vivid memories of our hauntings. We were never sure that they even knew when the lady was walking around and checking on the nursery, or when the heavy footsteps sounded outside. To the youngest children, the house was like one large play area. They were never menaced by the spirits, nor by our fears!

And the mansion? I never went back to the house, although I did drive by it several times while we still lived in the Philadelphia area. The house still stands, but the owners finally moved with the times. They decided it was too much house for one family and turned it into apartments. There was usually full occupancy in all the units—save one. One apartment always stayed vacant—the apartment which had been the lady's library!

ABOUT THE AUTHORS

HAROLD CAMERON and his family lived in the house on Plum Tree Lane for almost two years while he was sales manager for the Aluminum Company of America. He is presently the minister of the Paradise Church of Religious Science in Paradise, California, where he makes his home. He not only uncovered the ghostly mystery of the mansion on Plum Tree Lane, but he has also lectured on human relations at Philadelphia's Franklin Institute and has been chosen to write on sales motivation by the Harvard Business School.

CONSTANCE WESTBIE won the 1977 National Writers Club Award for Nonfiction for her collaboration with Harold Cameron in writing *Night Stalks the Mansion*. She met Harold Cameron while she was organist for his church in California and was so intrigued by the account of his experiences in the haunted house that she came out of a self-imposed retirement from writing to put his memoirs down on paper. Westbie's many fans will be glad to know that she is going to continue writing, having just completed a mystery, and currently writing a biography of Ingo Swann.

We Deliver!
And So Do These Bestsellers.